FEAST OR
FAMINE

Fred

FEAST OR FAMINE

*Teachings on
Mind and Emotions*

Lee Lozowick

HOHM PRESS
Prescott, Arizona

Cover design: Zachary Parker, Kadak Graphics
Layout and design: Kadak Graphics, www.kadakgraphics.com

Library of Congress Cataloging-in-Publication Data

Lozowick, Lee, 1943-
   Feast or famine : teachings on mind and emotions / Lee Lozowick.
      p. cm.
   Includes index.
   ISBN 978-1-890772-79-6 (trade paper : alk. paper)
   1. Thought and thinking. 2. Emotions. I. Title.
   BF441.L69 2008
   299'.93--dc22
                                          2008004584

HOHM PRESS
P.O. Box 2501
Prescott, AZ 86302
800-381-2700
http://www.hohmpress.com

This book was printed in the U.S.A. on recycled, acid-free paper using
soy ink.

08 09 10 11 12

To Yogi Ramsuratkumar,
without Whom the author of this book would be lost in a
morass, helpless and ignorant, no more nor less than one
bound hopelessly by illusion, tethered to the post of self-
centeredness, an ugly mass of turbulence and pain.

Oh Lord, Yogi Ramsuratkumar, Your lee is still all of these
things, but perhaps one degree less, by Your Blessings.

Our minds do not trust the Work. We have to bring our minds into alignment so that moment to moment we're saying *yes*. We've already said the big *Yes* or we wouldn't be here, but then we have to say *yes* every moment ... every day ... every week.

– Lee Lozowick

Contents

Preface

Mind? Emotions? What a mess. Hello. My name, in the basic three-dimensional reality that most of us subscribe to, is lee lozowick. I wrote this book, or rather I spoke it, and my fabulous editor put it together in comprehensible form, and yet I don't have the vaguest idea about what I have talked about and am even talking about right now in this Preface. Am I serious? Yes and no. Is that a serious answer to such an important question? Yes and no. What does that mean? I just told you that I haven't the foggiest. Where does that leave us? Good question and I truly believe that you may well get a step up on the answer by reading this book. So ... chop, chop (no, not wood and no don't carry water), time's a wastin', and as my mother used to say, "I could just plotz," so get on with it!

– lee lozowick
Prescott, Arizona
15 January 2008

Editor's Introduction

Lee Lozowick, whose considerations about mind and emotions are presented here, has been my spiritual teacher, my guru, for almost twenty-five years. I have the deepest respect for him and profound gratitude for the privilege of sharing his company. For all his enormous compassion to me and wide-ranging skillful means, which I have witnessed firsthand in countless circumstances, I don't hesitate to admit that he has been and is a hard teacher. Not only because he is uncompromising in his dealings with ego – in all its guises from arrogance to naiveté – but because he is often so maddeningly non-linear in his teaching style. The seeker or student who comes to this well to drink will first have to unravel the knotted ropes that keep the bucket secured. When his verbal teachings are transcribed from one of his public talks, for instance, his repartee with a questioner will occasionally read like the script of a stand-up comic. His stories will often roll on for pages, peppered with references to his heroes (from Bob Dylan to R.D. Laing to Charles Bukowski), with off-handed remarks about an old girlfriend in seventh-grade, only to be followed by extended and tender narrations of his encounters with his own beloved master, Yogi Ramsuratkumar – the beggar-saint of Tiruvannamalai, South India, who died in 2001.

Finding the "pointing out instruction" for how to work with mind, a phrase used in Buddhism which signifies a particular key to practice given to a ready student, is no simple task around Lee. One earns this pointing out instruction from this master by extreme patience, what might be better termed *endurance*. He does not *dispense* the teaching about mind, even though the practices he recommends are many and multi-leveled, as this book will delineate. Rather, he *is* the teaching about mind, which is why he is such a conundrum to the unprepared. His teachings are never crafted sermons. Rather, he allows his listeners (and in this case his readers) a window onto his own mind. His path to the center of an issue is more often than not circuitous; he talks *around* the issue, sometimes for a long time. He takes us on numerous side trips into past or future. He gets us laughing, uproariously even. We forget what the original point was, completely, only to have him jump out from behind the joke to surprise us with a gem of *dharma*, concluding his treatment, leaving his listeners breathless. In his ramblings, we see the machinations of mind, our own mind. We hear him admit to distractions and fascination, to arrogance, to curiosity and the love of "spiritual" gossip; and in the next breath we hear his declaration of absolute reliance upon the benediction of his master, Yogi Ramsuratkumar.

It is, of course, impossible for one who has not pierced the knot of the mind to ever judge or even fully understand the state of awareness of another. I see and judge everything with eyes and mind clouded with projections and expectations. That said, it is obvious that I cannot know the mind of my own spiritual master, nor fully appreciate his teachings about this subject, nor make any definitive statements about his intentions or his inner experience. Nonetheless,

I can point out numerous examples that possibly indicate a relationship to the mind that is quite different from mine, and from that of most of the world.

Observation is Key

Lee Lozowick's strongest teachings about mind and emotions are *not* contained on the pages of a book. Rather, they are found in the way he lives his life. Observing him – which can include observing his choice of language, or observation through listening to him in person– is how this teaching is received and understood. Observing *what he does* and *what he doesn't do*, along with noting the results that accrue from these *doings* and *non-doings*, is perhaps the most powerful approach to learning and absorbing the effectiveness of this way. Because readers of this book may not have this opportunity of first-hand observation, I will describe a few examples.

Lee Lozowick is constantly creating circumstances around himself that exact a high price in physical and emotional energy and attention from his students and devotees. In designing these circumstances, he also designs a built-in friction factory; a type of group work that pushes one to the limits of emotional endurance, while demanding a management of mind and intention that puts others ahead of self. At one time he initiates a rock and roll band, suggesting that they become "bigger than the Beatles" (it didn't happen). At another juncture on the path he forms a blues band and asks them to get themselves invited to the largest festivals in Europe (it did happen). Year after year he goes on pilgrimage in India with up to fifty travel partners, often including a group of infants or toddlers. He often asks that projects conceived of today be accomplished yesterday; and performances that would normally require years of practice be done with little or none. Spontaneity, it appears, is his favorite virtue.

Lee doesn't just talk about the dead ends that are implicit in conventional thinking. He is constantly *working with* the conventional barrier-creating mind of whatever group is closest to him at the time. He challenges group-think, media-mesmerism and middle-age stodginess at every turn, inviting individuals and groups to accomplish tasks that their rational minds alone would never allow them to begin. He asks one woman to take up blues harp and be ready to perform in a week. To another, who comes to him frustrated with her current work and wishing to break out, he recommends painting "bad art" and selling it for large sums of money. It doesn't matter to him that neither woman has any training or experience in these fields. (To the amazement of all, these two women pushed through their mind's initial *No* and surpassed everyone's expectations for what was possible; even Lee's!)

Close observation – between the lines – of Lee's published journals is another first-hand way to get his teaching on mind and emotions. For the past thirty-five years of his work, Lee has occasionally released his personal journals, which have then been published privately for use by his students. Each journal covers a period of several months, with one and occasionally two or three entries made on each day. For his own reasons, and much to our edification, Lee's entries are made *every* day, regardless of the circumstances of his life. He may be on the road with his band, or flying to Europe or India, or detained until nearly midnight with other duties. Still, he somehow manages to make the day's entry, even occasionally starting at 11:55 PM or a few minutes later. In these journals, he reveals that he holds himself to a no-editing rule. Whether the grammar or spelling is correct, or whether he makes his point in a way that is fully satisfactory to him, he puts these pages out to us, regardless, as they were initially written.

As an editor, easily frustrated with imperfect sentence structure, and as a devotee and student struggling with the machinations of mind as well as with inconsistency and lack of discipline, these journals are a cold lump of reality dumped on my dinner plate. What has always screamed out to me from these pages is Lee's seeming unconcern for his own mind's devious ways. "Devious" of course is my word. I still suffer mind's obsessions. Lee apparently does not; or if he does, he doesn't give credence to these obsessions by talking about them. Herein lies the teaching: It is not to be found in any technique suggested, primarily, but in the living witness that one does not have to take one's mind seriously; doesn't have to listen to its objections; and doesn't have to feel bad just because one gets distracted or even obsessed with something.

Reading Lee's context, rather than focusing on his content, I am confronted with a relationship to mind that upends mine. His journals are not *about* the teaching, particularly on the mind. Rather, as he has admitted in his own words, they *are* the teaching, a *koan* I've struggled with for years, editor that I am.

In the domain of his music, which he has been writing and performing for nearly twenty years, one finds that his rhythms and lyrics easily circumvent one's thinking and quickly generate new moods that were previously inaccessible; or they stifle old moods that had hung around for days. Attendees at his concerts report being captured by the wild enthusiasm of his performances, or moved to tears by his blues laments. Here is a teaching that captivates the body, taking participants to a place beyond mind, in the way that all great art can.

Whether one observes Lee packing a box of breakable objects, or laying out a table full of ages-old bronze artifacts, or structuring a typically no-free-time seminar, or hears him giving what seems like a stream-of-consciousness talk, or sees him handling his correspondence by writing on the empty spaces of magazine advertisement pages, the observant questioner will frequently find in Lee's simplest activities the answers they seek to the questions, "What is mind?" "What are emotions?" Lee himself put it this way when I questioned him at the start of this project: "Mind creates nothing but illusions and fantasies, and emotions suck. Okay?"

Working With This Book

"What is the nature of mind?" another student asked Lee in one of the talks included in this book. "That's too hard a question," Lee said, laughing, "Anything else?" He then proceeded to dive into the subject with gusto. His comments, on this occasion and throughout, are full of this hallmark of refreshing humor, serving as a constant reminder to relax. Yes, *relax!* he indicates again and again as he breaks the death-grip we have on our need to know. *Relax!* – perhaps the most vital instruction there is for working with mind, and certainly for working with this book.

The volume you have in your hands, if you read it carefully, *will* satisfy your need to know; and, between the lines, as in Lee's journals, you will stumble upon the non-linear teaching, a demonstration of the mastery of mind and emotion. You will find Lee's understanding of his own mind, based on acute self-observation; you will find clues to indicate a remarkably disciplined practice of attention; you may be startled by the creativity of a mind that isn't boxed in by convention; and you may be propelled, for a moment or two, beyond your own mind, for no apparent reason. Best of all, you may glimpse, as I did in studying these transcripts, that his attitude to mind is based in his surrender to God. By his own admission, particularly in the poetry he has written to Yogi Ramsuratkumar for decades (which is the subject of the *Afterword*), Lee presented his mind, heart, body, speech – all of it – to his master a long time ago. Mind, he says now, is no longer "mind" as we know it. Rather, mind is now Mind – inseparable from the knowledge and the being of the Divine. That said, a warning is in order.

The attempt to separate Lee's teachings about mind from his teachings about emotions, or from his teaching about faith or devotion or anything else would be an exercise in frustration. The teaching is one; the practice is holistic. We cannot work on emotions apart from working on the mind. We cannot investigate the nature of mind without encountering the emotions.

It is also not possible to isolate theory from practice, since Lee's teachings as contained here were most often given as responses to the questions – the immediate needs – of students or participants in his seminars. He rarely offers a purely theoretical consideration about anything. Such theorizing, I assume, would be a waste of his time. Unless the student had some background or experience allowing them to apply the theory, Lee would be speaking into a vacuum. His skillful means are generally too acute for that.

Because the topics addressed in this book were directed at individuals, there may seem to be many approaches to the same issue; some even contradictory. Closer examination, however, will reveal something else. With regard to handling strong emotion, for example, he may speak to one person about "sitting with what arises," while to another he suggests "doing something different, like moving the body." At bottom line, his considerations are not contradictory; they merely reflect the needs of different types of individuals, at different turns in the spirals of their practice.

The book is loosely structured, therefore. While one chapter or section may be titled *Self-Observation*, this subject is present in almost every other chapter as well. Another chapter may be called *Managing Attention*, but because this practice is integral to everything else, recommendations for working with attention are found throughout the book.

The reader is advised, therefore, not to attempt to further synthesize this teaching into precise sequence. Lee's teaching is circular, circuitous and holistic. Often it is "slogan based" – that is, his commentaries are often laced with practical teaching phrases, like "Draw no conclusions mind," or "Be that which nothing can take root in," or "Just this," or "Shut the fuck up." As Lee's editor, in the way I have grouped the essays, questions and fragments compiled here, I have already attempted to overlay some general progression to the teaching. The book starts with Lee's broad-brush definition of mind, and ends with his passionate plea for vigilance in the face of today's media-driven terrorism.

Each heading throughout the book designates one aspect of the teaching, often containing one or more valuable tenets. A teaching given by Lee in 1979 is often followed by a similar teaching from 2007, or the other way around. One of my great surprises in the editing process of this book was realizing how consistent this teaching has been from the beginning to the present day. It is not necessary, therefore, to read this book in order, although it may be useful to do so. Each essay, each section, offers a possibility for study and reflection that is not dependent necessarily on what comes before or what follows. And, everything is connected.

In some cases I have moved sections from one talk and incorporated them into another, in order to provide additional clarification or extended examples. In general, however, most of the material contained under one heading was given at one point in time.

Personal Note

I have no doubt that this particular book project was given to me because I needed it so badly. After over twenty years in my master's company I still went back and forth, sometimes daily, about whether his teaching about mind was "doing it" for me. I had read widely in Sufism, in Buddhism and in Christian mysticism. Every time I heard of a variation on some technique for meditation or self-observation, I tried to imagine how clear and centered and conscious I would be if only this practice were fully accomplished in me. The inner hell-realms created by dissatisfaction, by comparison, by needing to have the "most perfect" practice, and the "most enlightened" teacher, and all of it at once, were often overlooked for what they were – obsessions of my own mind; the results of a lifetime of neurotic perfectionism. Instead, these same states of anguish were often taken as signs that something was lacking in the teaching or in the teacher; while the states themselves remained basically unexamined. Working with the teachings contained in this book has uncovered many dimensions of my own personal hell.

I see now that one can wander the foothills at the base of the mountain for years, picking up interesting samples of flora and fauna, long delaying the fixing of one's sights on the path that is marked to the mountain's top. Dozens of techniques for mind practice and meditation can be collected. This book will supply many more. But, until one identifies the delaying strategy, and decides to stop the meandering, and actually starts using one or more of the methodologies or techniques, and applying it under *all* circumstances, and for years if necessary, one really has no grounds on which to determine its merits. May this book inspire such a decision is its readers.

My apprenticeship to Lee Lozowick in the domains of devotion and service has been, and continues to be, a slow process of burning through layers of procrastination, naiveté, fear and confusion. Transforming such reactive states into genuine compassion is one apt description of spiritual maturation. Apparently, it takes many of us a long time to grow up – sometimes, a *very* long time. For Lee Lozowick's continued commitment to witnessing to and serving this process in his students, I am deeply, deeply grateful.

Part I
MIND

CHAPTER 1

Taming and Training the Mind

What Is Mind?

Whenever someone asks for a definition of the mind I generally reply that this question is too hard for me, and "Do you have an easier one?" Because, you know, the mind is not just what thinks. It's more than that. Sometimes I use the words "mind" and "ego" interchangeably, but they're actually different things. And if someone asks me for my definition of what ego is, my answer is the same, "I don't know."

For the purposes of discussion we could say that "mind" (the way I use it), means that aspect of consciousness which believes itself to be independent and exclusive; and, based on that belief, creates the entire illusion of separation and identification.

The problem with life is not life itself. It is not the fact that there is pain, war, crime, aggression and violence. All of created existence flows between two poles – there is aggression, violence, cruelty and all of that, and there is also beauty, joy, delight, majesty, grandeur and nobility. The problem is that we identify specific things as if those specific things were who we are: "I am angry." "I am scared." "I am a good artist." All of that is identification, because all of those things arise and manifest, but none of them is who we are essentially.

So, the mind is the quality or characteristic of being that actually creates and sustains that illusion of identification. That's not a very satisfying definition for me, but it's a beginning.

We have mind. We have emotions. There are laws under which they function. And it is extremely important to direct both mind and emotions properly. If our minds and our emotions are running wildly and controlling us, instead of us managing them, then clearly any attempt to practice effectively, beyond a certain minimal level of maturity, is severely handicapped.

The unwillingness to deal with the mind (and we could call it "psychology" or "personality") interferes with practice, and also in a major way with professional success. This book is an attempt to set mind and emotions in context; to forcefully convey the need, in any situation, to establish the context whereby *we*, not *they*, are the masters.

Where to Start

We can only start from where we are. If where we are is that the mind is completely untamed, then we try to train it. If the mind is a "wild horse," which is a phrase used in Buddhism, or "wild monkey," the phrase used in Yoga, we can't train it until it's tamed.

A recent film, called *Flicka*, was about a man – a horse rancher – and his daughter, who was falling right into his footsteps. One day she saw this beautiful horse, a wild mustang, which she and her father then capture. The girl wants to train the horse, but her father has a reaction – he has been training horses all his life, since he was a little boy, and he tells her that she can't train a mustang; "They're completely wild." He tells her that she shouldn't do anything with the horse.

But, of course, she trains the mustang! In the middle of the night she goes to the horse's stall with a sugar cube in her hands. She stands some distance away and holds the sugar cube out. "Okay, if we're gonna be friends, then we're gonna have to come to this understanding," she says. "If you want this sugar, you're gonna have to come and get it. I'm not coming to you."

The horse comes, tentatively at first; but still it comes and takes the sugar. And this is parallel to the way we need to tame the mind.[1]

Training implies reliability. If we aren't reliable in our ability to feed back what it is that we're being trained *in*, then the training is at fault.[2] If the mind is untamed, then obviously you can still apply training, but you'll get random results: when the mind "feels like it," you'll get good results relative to the training, but when the mind "doesn't feel like it," because it's untamed, it will be like there never was any training.

Begin to tame the mind through self-observation, meditation, and rubbing up against the *koans*, like "Draw no conclusions mind."[3] You may have read about or heard that phrase. But, when you start observing the mind you will see the constancy of its conclusion drawing. So, you ask yourself, "What does it mean to have 'Draw no conclusions mind'?" "How do I do that?"

---

1 The Tibetan master, Chögyam Trungpa Rinpoche, used the phrase, "Take a friendly attitude toward your thoughts." In this same vein, Lee suggests that we approach our wild mustang mind with gentleness, rather than assume a posture of rigid control.

2 To "feed back" what we have been given means that we are able to articulate what we are receiving and practice what we are given.

3 "Draw No Conclusions Mind" is a phrase or slogan given by Lee to his students. It summarizes a way of working with mind. Lee refers to it here as a *koan*, meaning that the phrase needs to be chewed on, contemplated, until its truth is realized..

Technology for Taming

We actually don't have to have a technology to tame the mind because the mind essentially manages itself; it tames itself. What we need is instruction to convince the mind that it's better off tamed than untamed.[4]

The way we convince the mind that it's better off tamed than untamed is to gauge it against what we know to be wisdom. So, whether from Buddhist or Hindu scriptures, or the Christian desert fathers, there's a tremendous amount of wisdom relative to taming and training the mind, both. Keep rubbing up against *that*, and building intention. It's the intention that we build that gives the mind a willingness to tame itself. We could say "a willingness to *be* tamed," but really it's the mind that calms down and stops being unruly and says to us, "Okay, now train me," because the mind gets convinced that it's more profitable tamed than untamed.

Signs of the Untrained Mind, Untrained Emotions

Talking too much is one clear sign of a lack of management of mind. Talking too much in any capacity – like at the dinner table, just blathering on when you really have nothing to say. We see this with overselling. Insecure salespeople, even if they're very good at what they do, often have a tendency to not be satisfied when somebody says "Yes, I'll take it." The salesperson may just keep talking, and I've often been talked out of something I've already agreed to buy because someone keeps trying to sell me. This type of talking is such a waste of time and energy.

---

4 Lee is asserting that within his teaching there is not a formal "mind taming" practice.

A lack of management of emotions would show up as any kind of abuse or unnecessary aggression, whether it be talking aggressively to the waiter at a restaurant who accidentally brings us our steak too rare … or too well done … or without enough sauce … or with the sauce too liquidy … or with Alfredo when we ordered red sauce!

You may have seen somebody get out of their car, notice that their tire is flat, and then start kicking the tire as hard as they can. Any unnecessarily aggressive expression toward others, or things, indicates a mismanagement of emotions. Any reaction that lasts beyond a reasonable amount of time – being less than a minute, let's say – is another indication of the mismanagement of emotions.

Why Train the Mind?

Clearly, the pervasive influence of Yogi Ramsuratkumar's blessing organizes our world for us.[5] We simply find ourselves in the right place at the right time without thinking about it and without obvious indications. Our reality gets organized so that certain things are given to us as possibilities. We train the mind to be able to take advantage of all the blessing opportunities that come to us in recognizable form.

Once we have a certain possibility, then the training of the mind is useful, particularly if we want to be a musician, or an actor/actress, or a business person, or a corporate consultant, or a seminar trainer. The more trained the mind is, the more successful, in ordinary terms, we will be. If we

---

5 Yogi Ramsuratkumar (1918-2001), known as the Godchild of Tiruvannamalai, India, was a beggar-saint who lived the creed "Only God." He is Lee's spiritual master and the dynamic core around which Lee's teaching is built. When our lives are entrusted to God, through the agency of the guru, Lee says here, everything that unfolds in our lives is an expression of the Divine will.

want to learn an instrument and the mind is completely untrained, then it's necessary to have a teacher, a mentor, some framework in which we can plug in. But, if the mind is tamed and highly trained, then it's not out of the question that we could teach ourselves a musical instrument, and maybe go to a particularly proficient teacher for fine points and certain essential things that will be easier to get from an accomplished musician than to learn on our own.

The guitarist in one of our bands learned guitar by himself. His father hated his guitar-playing so much, because he had the idea that musicians were losers, that they never make any money. The young man used to have to hide his guitar under his bed or at friend's house so he could play without interference. If we want something badly enough, as this man wanted his music, we can often force the mind into a situation of being tamed and trained. But if not, it's useful to have training.

We're training the mind so that when we get an opportunity, instead of being naïve, we can see what's going on in the world around us. For instance, if we need to get tenure, we do what we need to do to get tenure to protect our job. That's what the trained mind does, instead of saying, "Oh well, I've been here for ten years, everyone loves me, no problem." When the university panics and needs money, it's a big problem, because you don't get a grant with a bunch of people who don't have degree letters after their names.

One of my students had to get a Ph.D. to advance as a teacher in the institute she taught for. She was going to go back to graduate school and do the whole bullshit trip, which I said was ridiculous. So she found a mail-order place, with a certified Ph.D. program. She went out to the place maybe twice a year for an oral exam, and the rest she did by computer. Once she got her Ph.D. degree she was smiled upon, of course. So, a trained mind will see what's needed and will handle what's necessary.

The average person – with the untrained mind – doesn't recognize value. He or she recognizes the herd instinct. When all the lemmings are running to the cliff, this person says, "There must be something good in that direction; that's why everybody's going that way." They jump on the band-wagon. It's herd phenomenon, it's not, "This is a valuable and useful situation."

The taming and training of the mind is essentially relative to a book that was out in the 1970s called *What to Do Until the Messiah Comes*. Ultimately, the taming and training of the mind fall away and are "out-brightened" by the radiance of Yogi Ramsuratkumar's blessing force. But, in the meantime, in order to optimize the opportunities of practice and to be able to most efficiently serve the Buddha, the *dharma* and the *sangha*, a trained mind is necessary.[6] For example, if the publicist for our press wants to keep selling books, and if our promoter wants to keep booking the bands, a trained mind is necessary. An untrained and untamed mind might get lucky once in a while. But what gives you the experience to know how to deal with booking agents or with people who are buying books is that the mind is trained, enough to have experience and to be able to capitalize on that experience.

A trained mind is useful to be able to handle the tremendous volatility of the world that we live in these days. Any of you who have traveled recently, I'm sure you've seen this at the airport. Everybody is pretty much prepared for a long

---

6 The Buddha, the *dharma* and the *sangha* are the "Three Jewels" in Buddhist cosmology. The *dharma* is the law or teaching and the *sangha* is the company of practitioners who practice the way together.

wait for security, but if the slightest extra tension is added, inevitably somebody in the line is going to freak out. And, have you seen the response of the security people the minute somebody starts getting pushy? Those security people are so afraid; they have been so beaten into the fear that somebody is going to shoot them or explode a bomb in their faces. When somebody starts getting pushy, the average security person totally panics. Their voice doubles in decibel-level and they instantly start threatening: "That's the law, that's the law! You can't …" They're absolutely hair trigger.

We live in a volatile world, and it pays to have a trained mind so that if you get upset about something you have enough sense to know that if you express that upset, you can get yourself in trouble. You can miss your flight; they can take you to "the room" and interrogate you, very easily. They'll let you go, eventually, because you're innocent of anything … except having an untrained and untamed mind! But, first they're going to keep you there for a couple of hours and bust your ass, because you picked on one of their employees, and anybody who works for the airlines sticks together.

Practice Wears Down the Mind

Dealing with mind and emotions all comes back to practice. In the most ordinary of circumstances, you want to have a trained mind so you can navigate your world in a way that optimizes your use of resources and energy so that you have the optimal amount for practice. We are training the mind to be more consistent and reliable in practice; and training the mind to optimize the energy and resources we have for practice.

One thing that practice aims toward is to establish us in a state of consciousness in which, while mind and emotions continue to arise, they then get allocated in whatever way is most useful, given whatever particular circumstance is most immediate. But, generally, we don't live in that condition.

When the sixteenth Karmapa[7] was dying he looked at his concerned disciples and said, "Nothing happens." If we were living in that state of consciousness, then, like the Karmapa, on our deathbed, when our disciples or families were freaking out in their minds and emotions, we could give them a word of advice, which is that "Nothing happens." We could give them something they could rub up against relative to their experience and relative to their faith in who we are as a senior practitioner, a parent or lover, or as a teacher, a saint or a sage, a Karmapa.

What the Karmapa's disciples could do was consider: "How could he say 'Nothing happens' when he was dying?" Good question! Maybe that's why he said that – to give them that kind of rub. If they were serious, they would solve the *koan* of "Nothing happens." Doing that, they would completely contextualize mind and emotions, which were obviously not running the Karmapa's consciousness, in any way, shape or form, when he was on his deathbed.

Practice wears down the mind. Remembrance wears down the mind. Every time you remember to do the heart breath,[8] every time you remember to do your beads, remember to chant, remember to enquire,[9] you are wearing down the mind.

---

7 Rangjung Rigpe Dorje, 1924-1981; the Karmapa is the spiritual head of the Karma Kagyu tradition of Tibetan Buddhism.
8 The heart breath is a specific practice given by Lee to his disciples; it is a method whereby one voluntarily works to transform the suffering of creation.
9 To "enquire" refers to the practice given by Lee to his students whereby one asks "Who am I kidding?" in relationship to the arising of any thought or emotion.

The mind is a forgetting machine when it comes to practice. Just remembering is a tremendously effective practice, which is why we say "Pay attention and Remember."[10] And, there is Remember with a capital *R* and remember with a small *r*. The practice is about both levels.

If you don't practice you won't be successful with the yoga. A primary element of the yoga is getting to a point where the mind does not run you.

Practice wears down the ego. And until our ego is in line with practice, basically you and I (meaning the guru) are going to be in a wrestling match with who is going to serve whom here. Ultimately. The Sufi teacher Irina Tweedie, when asked "What would you do differently if you went to your guru now, knowing what you know now?" simply said, "I would say Yes, right away." She was in her eighties; she knew she was going to die soon.

A student of mine died recently, and when everybody asked about him, I said he had a good death. Do you know why I said he had a good death? Because he was holding onto Yogi Ramsuratkumar for dear life, not holding onto his children, and not his ex-wives. He was hanging onto Yogi Ramsuratkumar, first.

God bless the man, because that's a fucking hard thing to do – to hold onto Yogi Ramsuratkumar's feet right up until the end. Usually, you know, you do it till it gets too bad. And when it gets too bad ... *whishst* ... Yogi Ramsuratkumar goes right out the window. And then you're screaming for your mother and your kids, and that girl in twelfth grade you could have slept with and you didn't. It all comes back!

---

10 "Pay attention and Remember" is another of the mind-training slogans used by Lee with his students. Obvious in its initial understanding, it is also a *koan* to be worked with.

But he just held onto Yogi Ramsuratkumar until the end. That was a good death. The best!

We are up against a mind that will not quit until it has to. A mind that will demand that everything that it has come here for be given to it. A mind that will put itself on the shrine, deify itself and demand for itself what we have found on the path in order to offer to God. That's what every one of our minds will demand. And if we do not confront that, deal with it, now … you do not want to be like Irina Tweedie on her deathbed, "What would you have done differently?" "I would have said yes right away." You want to say yes before, so it doesn't matter whether you would have said yes right away or not. You want to say yes now, so that by the time you get to your deathbed and someone says, "What do you regret?" You can't say, "my abject lack of practice … my resistance to the guru."

Who knows what you might regret? I think it will be back to the girl in high school for me. But, fortunately, the primary edict for my students is, "Do as I say, not as I do." Maybe that is why Gurdjieff wouldn't let anybody in when he was dying.[11] Maybe he lost it … Maybe that's why they never told.

Intention Is All

Training of the mind is a relative process, not an absolute process; but it is relative sometimes for lifetimes. We want to be very clear that, when we have a very highly-trained mind, as we understand mind, that when we die it goes – "it" is the

---

11 George Ivanovich Gurdjieff (1866?- 1949) was an Armenian-Greek mystic, a teacher of sacred dances, and a spiritual teacher. He is most notable for introducing "The Work," or as he first referred to it, the Fourth Way.

mind *as we know it* during our lives. Therefore, ultimately, the taming and the training of the mind lead back to a different kind of practice, not to more mental training.

Llewellyn Vaughan-Lee says, relative to psychology, that people don't have to be psychologically perfect, they just have to be basically mature.[12] He's come to the conclusion, as a teacher, that the amount of energy required to bring someone into "perfect" psychological balance is not worth the trade-off. As long as someone is essentially mature, that is, if they can manage their mind and emotions, that's good enough.

The training of mind doesn't necessarily lead to an obsessive heightening of mind – the approach one might follow if one were a particular kind of yogi or a tantric practitioner, in which you keep training the mind to more refined levels so that ultimately you can levitate, or create objects out of nothing, or bilocate ... all the fancy stuff. Our concern is that *the intention required to train mind carries through* to the next incarnation, so that next time it's much easier!

---

12 Llewellyn Vaughan-Lee, Ph.D., is a contemporary Sufi teacher and author.

CHAPTER 2

Self-Observation

In the spiritual traditions they often talk about this state of consciousness called "witness consciousness." There are three kinds of witnesses – ego, subtle witness (which is prior to or beyond ego), and the ultimate witness, in which there is no witness and nothing to witness, and yet there is still consciousness, still awareness.

Ordinarily, at the first level of witnessing, which is where we all start, it is ego watching whatever is going on. When we talk about "Paying attention," the instruction is: Pay attention to everything that arises, without judgment. Whatever arises: from the grossest level – like, you look at the sky, "Oh, there are no clouds; the sun is shining," or "I'm walking, I'm sitting, I'm talking" – to (with practice) the most subtle of manifestations, like experiences of telepathy; because there is a part of your mind that is telepathic with everybody, everywhere. But, because outer consciousness is discriminative, fortunately we aren't always knowing consciously all the things that we are receiving telepathically. Sometimes, particularly within families or couples who are very close to one another, when one person has something going on in the body (like a headache or a stomach ache) and they don't say anything, the other person feels it. One person's got a headache and the other person's got a sympathetic headache. It's not their headache. But they *think* it is theirs!

When we are instructed in the practice of self-observation, which is the same thing as "Paying attention," the instruction is: Don't value or judge what you're observing. Just see it completely impersonally. Because, the whole psychological dynamic of denial is about intentionally being blind to things we don't want to see about ourselves because they are either too painful or too ugly. Sometimes there are things that we do and we feel guilty about them. Instead of feeling guilt, however, we just imagine that we haven't done them, or we somehow change them in our minds.

Denial and Justification

"How come you're stealing postage stamps from your office?" you might ask someone. And the person replies: "It's not really stealing. I work every day there, and I'm a woman so I'm not paid as much as the man, who does the same work; he sits in the desk next to mine, but I get a lower salary than him. The *least* I deserve is postage stamps. It's not stealing."

That's how we justify things to ourselves.

For whatever reason, there are many things about ourselves we just don't like. If someone says to a mother who has lost her temper with her child, "Hey, why don't you relax, be more gentle, take it easy." She says: "That's easy for *you* to say. You don't have children. You don't know what it's like. You don't have a child asking you "why, why, why?' a thousand times a day." We justify our act of aggression in some way that is perfectly reasonable to ego.

In our community we have what we call "support groups." They usually end up being "attack" groups ... but the idea of a support group is that when somebody is struggling with some life issue, they can call together some members of the community and lay their struggle out. The other people are supposed to give them helpful feedback, or helpful advice. This is really a great idea in principle, but in practice it often works very differently, because often the person who asks for help doesn't want help, really. What they want is confirmation for their problem. They have a very specific idea of what kind of support they are willing to accept. And they will take only that kind of support.

I was in Paris years ago and a man asked me a question. He said: "I have this really big problem. My wife never wants to have sex. It's really a struggle for me. I want sex, and she never wants sex."

I said to him, "*You're* the problem." He looked at me like I was crazy. "No woman wants less sex than the man unless the man is the problem," I said.

He said, "Oh, in the beginning it was great, and now we've that been together for so much time, she doesn't want sex, and I do."

I said again to him, "*You're* the problem."

Oh boy, that really disturbed him. His wife probably told him that two-hundred times, and he didn't hear her once. But, he trusted me. I had some credibility with him. He didn't like the answer, but it was coming from me, so he was really trying to have some idea of what I was talking about.

We have some struggle in life, some crisis, whatever it is, and we want help, but we have to be willing to take help objectively. There are things that we don't like that we just completely justify and excuse. But, when we are talking about paying attention, we have to see every quality of every moment clearly, without denial or justification or analysis, without editorializing, without guilt, without shame. And, the way paying attention begins is with the ego – always, with everybody, unless you're born a saint. (I certainly wasn't. I know some teachers who say they were born enlightened, and that they intentionally forgot that they were enlightened so that they could experience ordinary life, before they reentered their constant state of enlightenment so that they could teach. It's a great line. I wish I could use it. But I'd feel like so much of a hypocrite that I'd hate myself in the morning.)

First Step

The first step in working with mind and emotions is practical self-observation. You might want to make a checklist: What's the first thing you think of when you get up in the morning? What's the first thing you think of when you look in the mirror in the morning? What's the first thing you think of when you go to your closet and you're trying to pick out what shirt to wear?

These are real, immediate, practical ways to practice self-observation. Observe your responses in these situations. What story are you telling yourself? What's going on? When you can't find the shirt you want is the first thing you think, "Jesus! my fucking life is … !" What's the first reaction you have on a basic ordinary level?

When we talk about self-observation usually we think, "Oh well, I've got to observe myself clearly so I can see my greed." But, what about the way you drive? Self-observation starts at the grossest, most basic level. Do you ever observe yourselves driving a car? That's a perfect place to start. How fast do you drive? How are you in relationship to other drivers? Any kind of traffic situation is a prime place for self-observation. If you're a passenger in a car and you're observing yourself, what's your mind doing relative to the other driver? You know you're going to be either praising or criticizing the other driver, unless you're just daydreaming the whole time. But most people who are passengers in a car, particularly with someone they don't know well, are busy paying attention to the road in case they have to avoid an accident from the passenger side of the car. Self-observation applies in whatever you do. Not that you stop doing all that, but you just observe yourself doing it!

Start self-observation in a place anybody can relate to. Or, if you are a dyed-in-the-wool Pollyannaish positive-thinker, a good mentor can design self-observational questions like, "Are there any negative aspects to circumstances that you try to think positively about?" Such a question requires actually having to look at the process of the mind. Are you denying, or repressing, or being honest about what you're perceiving when you think positively, or when you try to use positive affirmations?

Our self-centeredness is so habitual that we are totally unaware of the fact that when we put the *prasad*[13] in our mouths we drop the wrappers on the ground. Our self-observation is so blind to our own habits. Our idea of self-observation is, "Well, everybody is the same, so I'll observe so and so, and write the spiritual master long letters about all of their problems."

On my ashram in Arizona we have an old ceramic toilet in the flower bed outside the *darshan* hall.[14] It is a reminding factor; a dramatic, in-your-face example of who we are and

---

13 *Prasad*: an offering, a gift; an exchange of gifts between guru and devotee. In this case Lee is referring to the small wrapped candies that he distributes to devotees following meditation and during the Sunday formal *darshan*.
14 *Darshan* hall is the formal space in which the guru or master meets with his or her students or disciples.

how we treat the ashram. There are countless examples of disrespect of the ashram, from leaving dirty dishes in the sink, to our relationship to food, to our anger that we have to bring receipts back when we get petty cash. It could be to anything. Those kinds of things are glaringly disrespectful to the ashram, to the path that you've chosen, and disrespectful to the Work![15]

Do you know who you are? Do you know that you drop *prasad* wrappers on the ground without even thinking about it? Do you know that you drive in an aggressive, chip-on-your-shoulder manner? Do you know that every time you refer to gays, blacks, Jews, Arabs, obese people, old people, whomever, there is a tone of bias, disgust, bigotry, superiority, whatever, in your voice? Do you know why? That's the whole purpose of self-observation, not to make a moralistic decision and stop doing those things and then get some rash on your body because you're not driving like a maniac in traffic anymore. Self-observation is to reveal your judgments, and all the veils you use to cover yourself; it is to see yourself *as you are.*

Change *will* happen. The Work *will* take care of change. You don't need to worry about that. All you need to do is see yourself nakedly!

In fact you might try that. Take off all your clothes (this is no "spiritual" thing, any Gestalt practitioner can tell you this) and just stand in front of a mirror, and look at yourself. And give it about an hour. Not like, "*Oo-oui*, I need to take care of those thighs!" But just look at yourself: every crease, every wrinkle, every mole, every freckle. Look there,

---

15 Work, with a capital W, refers, in many spiritual traditions and recently in the teachings of Gurdjieff, to the Work of God in which human beings are called to participate.

on your beautiful arm, the one that your lover is always kissing and licking every chance they get, is a big hair about three inches long. And we wonder, "How the hell did *that thing* get there overnight? It wasn't even there when I went to bed at night, and there it is, sticking out, long, black as the devil's asshole." And you rip it out ... and you look at the thing and you go, "Life! Isn't life amazing! That damn thing grew overnight. Amazing."

We pull that hair out because somehow it is inconsistent with our image of ourselves.

Make a Decision

In the beginning, when you start paying attention, because it is just ego that is paying attention, of course we are going to be selective. We are going to see some things very clearly, and some things we're not going to see at all. That's the way we all begin. We start there. But, if we're really committed to the practice of paying attention ... and how do we get committed to such practice? Make a decision!

My ex-wife, before we got together, was an alcoholic, smoked two to three packs of cigarettes a day. She was a "warrior" so she didn't smoke filtered cigarettes. She worked during the week, and she and her husband at the time (they were both alcoholics) would go out every weekend and get totally blind, unconscious drunk; and they'd stay drunk the whole weekend. Then, on Monday morning, she'd wake up, sober herself up for the week, and go to work. That's the way they lived their lives.

We both attended the same weekend course, the Silva method (of which I later became an instructor). In that first course she got into a state of meditation, and had a very clear picture of her life as it existed before this weekend. She saw clearly how completely inelegant, undignified and disrespectful toward herself she was being. And she came out of the state of meditation and said to herself, "I'm never going to smoke or drink again," and she never did.

That decision created a divorce, because her husband would not stop drinking or smoking, and all of a sudden he had no partner, because that was what their life was all about. She had no struggle, no temptation. She made a decision, and the decision was made so conclusively that she walked out of that room and never had the urge to drink or smoke again. That was over thirty years ago. As far as I know, she hasn't picked up a cigarette, and doesn't take a drink, and doesn't miss it. It means absolutely nothing to her. It's kind of like a miracle story because she'd spent ten years getting blind drunk every weekend. She was an alcoholic, and in one momentary decision, it was severed.

How do we commit to the practice of paying attention, or any other practice? Make a decision. How do we know that the decision is effective? It doesn't matter. This is the thing, and it's a very important point. *It doesn't matter!* If you are a person of integrity, a man or woman of integrity, you make a decision and you just stick by the decision.

Many of you, at random times in your life, have had the urge to lie or steal, or worse, but you didn't do it? Not because you couldn't do it, or because you didn't want to do it, but because you made a decision: lying is not just; stealing is not just ... that's all. And, in spite of temptation, sometimes really strong temptation, when you could steal and know for sure that you wouldn't get caught, still you don't anyway, because you made a decision. It's exactly the same with spiritual practice

The point is, whether the decision is objective, whether the decision to practice was made from the deepest essential core of your being, or whether it was just some impulsive psychological mistake you made, it doesn't matter. You make the decision, you stick by the decision. It doesn't matter if you *feel like* doing something else. You don't refrain from doing something because you're afraid of being punished or caught. You simply don't do the action, because you have innate, "intrinsic dignity" (Prajnanpad). Every single human being has intrinsic dignity. But often not being in touch with that, being conscious of that, we act in undignified ways.

So, when you hear this consideration, "Pay attention," we all start from the same place. What hears "Pay attention?" Ego. What manifests "Paying attention"? Ego. And so, in the beginning you're selective. We notice certain things and we don't notice other things, and it's completely strategic, but unconscious. In our conscious mind we imagine that we're observing everything, we're paying attention to everything. But we're not.

The Threads and the Roots

When we haven't rooted out the subtle threads of egoic motivation we can look so good on the surface that we don't even know these subtle threads are there. Until our life circumstances serve to brush away the grass on top of the water, we don't see that there is anything going on underneath. Not seeing what is going on underneath, we assume there isn't anything. Or, to use another example, we may see the ashes of a fire and see that they are not smoking: "Oh, great, the fire's out," we say. When, in fact, underneath the ashes there could be burning embers.

The practice of self-observation is the clear awareness, that needs to be sustained, which notices when those subtle potentialities are present. In noticing them, it also notices when we are hooked by them; in noticing that we are hooked, it doesn't need to allow their manifestation to happen. If you don't know that those subtle manifestations are present by the time you are hooked, you are already manifesting the habit. If you know they are there, and you're noticing them whenever they kick up dust, then when the hook comes in it won't engage. Your action won't *need* to follow the mental image. But if you don't know they are there, your action will follow the mental image. By the time you've caught it or noticed it, you've already created the karma, or reinforced the habit, or put your foot (or hoof) in your mouth ... whatever it is that we do.

In Tibetan Buddhism they would study the *abidharma* in order to develop a clear, at least intellectually, picture of the way the mind works.[16] In the practice of self-observation as I teach it, we haven't defined that formal a technology. We say, just observe yourself at all levels, subtle and gross. We start, of course, with the gross level, which is obvious: We see ourselves the way we are in relationship; the attachments we have relative to money, food and sex. When that's really obvious, when we know ourselves pretty well – we know our predictability and mechanicality – then we start observing feelings, and the emotions that are associated with the actions (which of course we are doing all along, anyway). For example, you're at the end of the line for lunch and something really good is on the buffet. You're afraid that you're not going to get any; that it will be all used up by the time you get to the front of the line. Here the action is very

---

16 *abidharma*: Sanskrit, meaning the higher dogma or doctrine.

clear. You start associating emotions and feelings: Are you just greedy and frustrated, or are you angry at the person in the front of the line? Are you mentally projecting, "Don't take so much"?

You follow all of the internal associations, along with the gross external behavior, and then you start noticing the subtle connections. For instance, in another case, perhaps you thought that you were motivated to bring clarity to a circumstance, when in fact your real motivation was to give your own child an advantage in any given situation. That is the kind of subtle inner motivation which we usually don't apply to ourselves. We want to think that we have higher ideals; that our motives are more oriented to right dharma and right behavior; right relationship and all of that.

There are many levels of self-observation. What we are talking about here is that once you've had the experience of clear, objective self-observation, you know what the subtle cues are. You have a sense of the way your inner system works. Then you need to sustain that realization so you don't keep getting hooked.

Articulate Your Aim – A Practice of Self-Observation

From his Paris talks during the war, Gurdjieff is quoted as saying is that our neuroses are "dogs." If our neurosis is pride, or vanity, or greed, or rage, or whatever it is, he said, "That's your dog." And, he said, we have to fight, because these qualities in us have been crystallized in us as children, based on a certain interpretation we made; the only inter-pretation that a child *can* make, because a child can't think with an adult intellect.

We imply certain things from our experience and then we make certain leaps of judgment; and those things become the laws by which we live as adults. We may decide that food equals love, and as adults we may have various neurotic relationships to food because as a child the formula "Food is Love" is crystallized in us. Gurdjieff said that as adults we demonstrate that these qualities crystallized in us as children.

Our ashram once received a gift of a large amount of cane sugar (two or three hundred pounds), and we had it around for a long time, because we don't use sugar that much. So, after awhile, some of the sugar solidified, and literally it was hard as a rock. We chipped it with an ice pick and nothing happened. We had to boil it in water, for hours, just to get it to de-crystallize. So, when Gurdjieff talks about "crystallization," that's what he's talking about. Something solidifies to such tenacity that by the time we're adults, when we discover the Work, trying to fight against that crystallization without outside help and extraordinary discipline must be a losing battle.

Gurdjieff says that when we discover what our "dogs" are – or what our dog is, what in Fourth Way terminology might be called "chief feature"[17] or "chief weakness" (or Gurdjieff would probably have called it "chief dog") – the power of our crystallization, the power of our neuroses, is so strong and so sophisticated, that we're in a tremendously weak position in relation to it. That's just the way it is. The tremendous emphasis, force and remembrance that we have to bring to dealing with this thing, for most people is impossible. Most

---

17 "chief feature," term from Gurdjieffian work, which refers to the organizing principle of the personality; it remains hidden to the personality, but is generally obvious to others. Identification with this principle keeps us from experiencing the waking state.

people simply won't do it. Everything in us will try to sabotage the fulfillment of those functions we have in this Work.

Gurdjieff says that *everything* in nature will fight against the Work, and try to sabotage and undermine our steps forward. Whatever our role or post is, whatever our task is in this lifetime in the Work, everything in us will fight against *that*; will convince us that "it's not so"; will convince us that we're being egotistical and arrogant to even think such things; that we can't do it; that we're being completely fantastical and superstitious ... whatever the case might be. We will even fight physically, not just intellectually and emotionally, against our accomplishment of the task.

Gurdjieff says that, when you have a clear moment (and we all have clear moments now and then; moments when we know the reality, the truth of things), *you have to articulate that moment*. He talks about it in terms of "defining an aim," or setting a goal, having a wish. You have *to articulate it in that moment*, because that moment is soon going to be gone, maybe, literally, in the next instant.

An interesting example of what can happen in a clear moment happened to the preacher Jimmy Sweigert. In a book about him the author reported that when Sweigert was ten years old he fell into an altered state of consciousness that fundamentalists call "prophesying," and which the biographer called a genuine state of religious transformation. It lasted for three days. During this time, which was in 1945, about a week before they dropped the first bomb on Hiroshima, he was prophesying. One of the things he said was that a large bomb, unimaginable to most of mankind, would be dropped very soon.

Sometimes our state of opening lasts for days, sometimes even months. But, ordinarily, it's there and gone. Literally, we have this instantaneous experience: reality opens and we see the truth, not only universally, but personally; we see our role, our path, our destiny. Much like how, just in the instance that someone dies, their whole life flashes before them. Our moment of clarity might only be a half-second of clock time, but in that half-second we see the whole thing. We see who the guru is to us; we see the Work; how our whole life was designed to bring us to the point of meeting the teacher, stepping on the path, entering upon the process. And it's amazing! And, in an instant it's gone.

Gurdjieff says that when you see that, you have to act quickly – while it's fresh in mind, before nature comes in and totally manipulates the whole thing, taking it over and using it against us, making us think we're a new prophet and going to start a new religion (that's how nature takes our glimpses of reality and turns them against us). You have to *articulate what you know to be true about the Work, and, in particular, about your personal process.* Then you have to repeat that articulation to yourself ten times, one hundred times, a thousand times, a million times. The first ten times it won't make any difference; the first one hundred times it won't make any difference in terms of the complete domi-nation that your habits have over you. But, sooner or later, if every time the habit comes up, you say to yourself (as you have articulated it): "I'm identified with those things. I am not those things," sooner or later, the 101st time, the 110th time, the 500th time, you're going to say it and all of a sudden the habit is going to be completely obscured in that moment, completely. And you *will be* controlling the assertions! Your unitive "I" will be in control.

This realization might go away in the next instant. But, in the moment you have it, instead of being completely a slave to your habit (in which case nothing you do can move it; you go on meeting the stimuli in life and reacting totally like a machine), if you keep stating what you *knew to be true* in that moment of genuine, objective clarity, sooner or later you will be in control and the habit will be a slave to you. You'll know it, and that knowing it will give you strength, and power. Each time *that* happens, the habit being your slave becomes stronger and stronger. At a certain point, maybe it may take years, *you* have more power than the habit. And then, instead of you being the slave of the habit, the habit becomes your slave, permanently, and that's when you take a leap forward in the Work.

What often happens is that we have a very genuine, objective realization but we forget it in an hour, or a day or two, or a week. Then the habit snaps right back into place. The practice of self-observation in any system is such that, once you have pierced the confusion and the lack of clarity, and you *have* clarity, you don't ever want to go back to a place in which the things that you have clarity about are manipulating you. You want to remember those things and continue to see those things, up to and until the point, and through the point, where those things are not actively engaging any more.

This will come, in time. If you are denying the engagement of the hook, then, over some period of time (depending upon the individual it could be months or even years), the "thing" – the habit – will stop working. Ultimately, that's your aim. The thing stops hooking, so that your behavior can be just, and aligned with the Work and the dharma, instead of manipulative and unconscious. Self-observation is an absolutely core and essential practice.

Going Deeper

A student recently asked me about the bind he was in. He saw that he was identifying with his effort of self-observation; feeling good about his practice of not acting on his habit. I responded that just as the practice of self-observation becomes deeper and deeper, so too our attachments become more and more sophisticated. Chögyam Trungpa Rinpoche talked about spiritual pride being one of the final domains of spiritual materialism. I would say that the attachment to "right practice" in any form, not just to self-observation, tends to be one of the domains that we assume unconsciousness about, because the result of right practice *is* the result we are aiming for. (And if you have to choose the "best" attachment to have, "right practice" would certainly be the best attachment!)

As we are self-observing, the attachment to our efforts tends to come at the end of the process because we just take it for granted: "Well, I have to make effort," we say. Yet, we overlook the fact that we've given substance to the effort to right practice, instead of including it in the field of all phenomena of dependent origination[18] and essential insubstantiality. We see this readily with solid phenomenon. You can knock on a piece of wood and say, "Oh, this is originally dependent and insubstantial." It's easiest to come to that realization about physical things, and then with emotional things ... but then it gets more and more sophisticated.

Zen master Soen Sa Nim [Seung Soen] used a great example (in a recent article of his writing in a current Buddhist

---

18 Dependent origination (*pañicca-samuppàd*) describes a view of life in which everything is interconnected. Nothing is separate, nothing stands alone. Everything "depends" for its origination on something/everything else.

magazine) about someone who gets jealous, is in a complete emotional tizzy, and then realizes that the perceptions he was basing this jealously on were misperceptions. All of a sudden the jealously goes away! Soen Sa Nim used that as an example of how you gradually come to the realization of the insubstantiality of emotional reactions. You look at how your emotions depend on a certain catalyst, and you see that if the catalyst is not there, no reaction. If the catalyst is there, reaction. And if you see the catalyst a different way, all of a sudden what was completely substantial in one second is completely gone and insubstantial in the next second.

So, we move through the observation of the original dependent origination and insubstantiality relative to gross physical things first, that's the easiest thing. Then, we move on to feelings and emotions, and we keep observing subtler and subtler attachments. If somebody is attached to a new car, that's pretty obvious; or someone has attachments to certain kinds of food or looking a certain way, dressing a certain way. We can figure those things out very easily. But, then there are the attachments at subtler and subtler levels.

Love, for example, as a feeling or a mood, tends to be so nebulous anyway that we would not think that we had any attachments to it. We say, "I know how fleeting love is and how insubstantial," when actually we make plenty of attachments relative to subtle relationships to our friends, family, children, partners.

As self-observation deepens we see the subtler and subtler attachments. And one of the last ones we see is that we've actually attached to the practice of self-observation, because the automatic assumption is, "This is right practice, I'm just naturally and spontaneously practicing," when actually we've developed an attachment. It's a matter of not stopping practice too soon. Like in the Lyings process[19] developed by Swami Prajnanpad,[20] there are several levels of realization, and every level of insight feels the same. Meaning that, when we break open a certain illusion the realization feels final. Even at the most superficial level, when we really see an attachment "as it is" we say "Ah, I'm free." When, in fact, all we've seen is the first level.

Often Swami Prajnanpad would recommend ongoing sessions of Lyings because people would assume, having had one breakthrough, that they didn't need another. They assumed they were finished because the clarity of what they were seeing was so freeing and so revealing that there was an automatic assumption, "Ah, that wasn't so bad. I'm done."

Swami Prajnanpad has shown, in his experience, that when people go into the next level they have a deeper realization. And that realization feels exactly the same way. Then they say, "Oh, I'm glad I didn't stop. But now I'm done."

One of the reasons you do Lyings with a coach or mentor is because the outside observer has a better sense of whether you actually have come to the end or not. "But, I've had this profound realization. I now understand all this extraordinary stuff," the person may say. But there may still be the very subtle connections.

Soen Sa Nim notes that when you are a baby you are essentially pure sensation: you're cold, you're hot, you're hungry. And, as a baby, you react purely instinctually based on these sensations. Nevertheless, you are still making subtle

---

19 Lyings is a type of psycho-spiritual process developed by Swami Prajnanpad for working with psychological blocks. The process is so-called because the participant lies down during the session.

20 Swami Prajnanpad (1891-1974), the Bengali spiritual teacher whose teachings were first encountered and brought to the West in the 1960s by French seekers Arnaud Desjardins and Daniel Romanoff.

associations all the time, but you don't know it, because the thinking mind is not engaged yet. You don't have reflective thinking. As adults, however, we're so identified with our referential thinking domain that, when we have an insight that we can language, we think, "That's it. I've made all the connections. I've rooted out all the associations." Because at some level we have. But to really practice ultimately, we also have to feel those subtle attachments that we made in pre-referential thinking. And those can be so deep and so subtle that most people would never think to continue a practice beyond a certain feeling of emotional insight. They would never continue to the level of the pre-emotional and primal. Yet we have to sustain the practice!

The challenge is that you won't recognize what these pre-associations are. You don't see them coming. You only recognize what they were when you've detached from them. By the way you are functioning, you recognize that you have rooted out those subtle attachments.

It's a type of "*Oh my God*" realization: you see it in a way that doesn't have descriptive or intellectual associations at all. Also, they may be so subtle that you may not have an obvious feeling association. Yet, you see it *as it is*, and the seeing is undeniable. But there may be no major physical sensation associated with it. It's a tacit realization.

One of my students noticed that when he got up after meditation practice at the ashram and was walking to his car he was moving differently; "… like a sane person," he said. That's a good example of what we've been talking about. When you have no intellectual description for what has been touched, but the change is obvious – like in the way you walk or move – that's deep! It may not be that you've arrived at the bottom of the barrel as far as your attachments are concerned, but you're really getting down there. What enables this realization to be sustained is living in the ongoing state of meditation in which it arose. The tendency is, however, that we get up from meditation, we get busy ... and that state of clarity is completely put away until the next session of meditation. But, fortunately, those events are cumulative, although obviously the longer the time period in between active periods of practice, the more dusty and hidden away they become. If you go away for a couple of years and you try to remember where you put everything in your room, often you forget. It's a similar process. So you want to keep this state fresh, as much as possible.

Know Your Character

E.J. Gold[21] says that there are many characters[22] in us, including the "disciple." And we can choose which character we're going to animate. So, if a character is being animated that is not the character that we would like to be animated (like the "saboteur"), it is possible to choose another character. Because, if somebody said to any of us, what are the qualities of a disciple, for example, there would be various differences in our answer, but most of us would have a pretty clear idea of how we would define "disciple." In a technical sense, it is just as easy to animate the "disciple" character as it is to animate the "saboteur" or the "rageoholic."

---

21 E.J. Gold – contemporary author, shaman, spiritual teacher, in the tradition of the 4th Way; founder and teacher of the IDHHB, Institute for the Development of the Harmonious Human Being, based in Grass Valley, California.

22 character, as the term is used by Mr. Gold, refers to the role one takes up or position one assumes when engaging in a video game. One takes on a certain "character" with all its attributes, strengths and weaknesses, weapons of defense and so on, and then proceeds to play the game as that character. When the game is finished, one can take on another character.

The more intimately you know any other character, the easier it will be not to allow that character to interfere. So, it's back to ruthless self observation.

When a character arises, like the saboteur or rageoholic, the way you get to know it better is to see it, with no justification, without trying to pretty it up in any way. If you are trying to disguise it, then also you are not coming to know it intimately. The more intimately you know that character, the less that character will surprise you or manipulate you or dominate you. So, whenever that character arises, instead of fighting it, or trying to run away from it, or pretending it's not there, you accept it completely *as it is*, and in that acceptance you see the character as it is. When something is seen that clearly it doesn't have the same power. It can't sneak in and take over when you are unprepared. Because you know its sneaky ways. You've seen it. If one of your relatives is a heroin addict, and you know it, and they've been an addict for a while, you know every excuse that they can possibly use to use *you* to get drugs. So when they call you up with the excuse, you already know it's an excuse; you know it because you know the way they work.

It's the same with any one of your interior characters. If you *know* the character, then the character can't take advantage of you. Which is why, when the character arises, you want to *see* it instead of avoiding it. Once you know it intimately, it won't have the same function. It will not!

No Momentum Needed

The beginning of work-on-self is self-observation. This is a foundational level of practice for many different paths. This practice doesn't require momentum because you don't build up to a goal. Rather, you practice in the moment. So, the phrase used by Arnaud Desjardins[23] for the internal process is "actively passive." You simply observe, without having to do anything that requires effort. Or, we could say it's an effort of attention. You do have to pay attention, but paying attention takes place in complete sympathy with whatever else you're doing in the moment, including sitting on the couch watching television, being lazy.

As I've mentioned before, when in the act or process of seeing clearly, the answers that we often search for are often right there, and obvious. For example, you can struggle against laziness by trying to motivate yourself, or putting little positive signs all over the place: "Get up and work you lazy slob," or whatever. Or, you can recall a nice little Zen story about work.

There was once an old Zen master whose practice was to work in the field every day. As he got older, his well-meaning community thought, "Oh this poor old guy, he's such an old man, he's been working so hard all his life, he serves us so much, he deserves to rest." So the board of directors got together (or however they did it then, since this was over one-hundred years ago) and made a law that this guy had to stop working.

In his wisdom, the Zen master thought it was better idea to obey the board of directors than to put up a fight, so he stopped going to the field. And at the next meal, he simply sat. When food was served to him he didn't eat. The students thought that maybe he was not feeling so well, so they didn't pay much attention. But, every time food was served for the next couple of days, he didn't eat.

---

23 Arnaud Desjardins, a contemporary French author, filmmaker and spiritual teacher, whose ashram, Hauteville, is located in southern France. Desjardins is a disciple of Swami Prajnanpad, and a close associate of Lee Lozowick.

After awhile, of course, the students got worried and somebody asked the old monk if he was sick, or if there was a problem with the food. He said something to the effect (and I can't quote it exactly because it was in archaic Japanese), "If I'm not working I'm not earning food, so I won't eat." Hearing that, his students (as they say in the story) were then all enlightened and they let him go back to the fields.

So, maybe if somebody is inspired by the Zen story they'll put a little sign on the refrigerator, "No work, no food." But, when it comes to inner work, we don't have to build momentum and psyche ourselves up and get ready for it. In the outer world, everybody prepares for whatever it is they are going to do in a different way. Like Barbra Streisand, fantastic singer, gets ready for every show by throwing up, because she's so nervous, terrified to go out in front of people and sing, even though she's been doing it for forty years, and she's got a gorgeous voice, and fantastic stage presence. Or, you see boxers, before going out in the ring, sort of psyching themselves up. Like Mohammed Ali, one of the greatest boxers of the twentieth century. He was like an animal. Like a lion. What a body! If I didn't like woman so much I would have been in love with Mohammed Ali. That guy was gorgeous at his peak. Well, he used to walk around going, "I'm the greatest, I'm the greatest ..." psyching himself up. But, to practice, you don't have to do any of that stuff. You don't have to psyche yourself up, or make preparations, or build momentum. Even though some of you probably do. You probably get ready to come to your retreat at Hauteville[24]: "*Next week* I'm going to observe myself. *Next week* I'm going to accept what is as it is. *Next week*, I'm gonna say *Yes*."

---

24 Lee is speaking to the students at Arnaud Desjardins' ashram, Hauteville, in southern France.

But, in fact, practice requires no preparation. It's back to the NIKE slogan, "Just do it!" (Unless you're a thief, then "Just *don't* do it!")

CHAPTER 3

What Possesses You?

One of the primary aspects of sadhana is to self-observe to the point where we have some sense of what we are possessed by. Obviously, if you have a professional passion and you have a certain goal for your professional life, but you're not relaxed about it, and it is really driving you, that's a kind of possession. Or, if you are fixated on someone who has died – either you haven't grieved properly or you don't grieve – and you allow your attachment to that person to completely control you, that's being possessed. Because if you grieve properly, your grief might take a week, it might take a month, it might take a year, but eventually you would finish your grieving. Certainly you will always remember that person, fondly, but you'd be finished with the grieving. Of course that applies on the negative side too. If someone dies and you've had a negative relationship to them, instead of a loving relationship, and you maintain a constant association with that negativity, even after the person's died, that's a form of possession. We need to self-observe to the point where we have a sense of what possesses us.

A lot of us are secretly possessed. We don't know we're possessed because we think that we've given up whatever it is! For example, you think you've given up coffee, and you are convinced that you've given it up. You haven't had coffee in years, because of your discipline and your commitment

... and all of a sudden, we start getting more coffee here than we can drink (because two new students have a coffee shop in town) and we're drinking coffee all the time. There are people who have not had coffee in years who are still completely possessed by the coffee entity. And the minute we started having coffee again it was as if they had never given it up. They were right back there.

So, very often we have passions of our youth and we don't know we are still possessed by them. They are buried. As we get older, we get wiser; we've learned our lessons. We think we are not possessed anymore by the passion of our youth, and we often find out when that thing comes back into our life, if it does, that this possession is still there – the same need, the same impulsiveness, the same lack of clarity and distinction.

It is particularly important that we self-observe about what possesses us so that when we have to deal with that thing we have some degree of consciousness about it, which gives us some degree of choice. Because as long as we don't know what we are possessed by, we have no choice.

People get astrological charts done because they figure that if they know what's coming they can strengthen themselves emotionally; they can prepare for it. Since most astrological signs are indications and potentialities, not written-in-stone absolutes, there is a very real possibility that if you knew your astrological indices you could, if not *avoid* certain things, minimize certain things. In many cases, knowledge is useful. And, with the knowledge that we have certain strengths and certain weaknesses, we could play on our strengths and strengthen in things that are weaknesses. So, we should want to know what possesses us.

It is said that the influence of our heritage goes back seven generations. That's a lot! Most of us didn't know our great-grandparents at all; maybe they came from another country. We know nothing about ancestors back that far. And yet, in the chemical structures of our body, literally, not in some kind of mind memory, but in the chemical structure of our cells, there is pretty consistent agreement that we are influenced by seven generations back. That's pretty startling, especially if you come from a family of murderers, thieves, rapists, bigots and inquisitors. That the influences of people whose lives were completely dominated by the drive for power and authority, control, and wealth, are affecting you, is pretty startling.

It can be not only useful, but protective, to the ongoing health of your commitment to the path, to have a sense of what you are possessed by. For example, if you know you have a weak spot for fame, and somebody offers you some fantastic opportunity to be famous, if you know that that's what possesses you, you might have enough presence of mind to actually think logically about what they are offering you. You may realize that until something is signed, and until you meet the actual people that you are going to be dealing with, and until the circumstance has been financed and has the resources collected to actually *do* the thing that this whole fantastic idea is based on, you've got nothing but air. And if you don't have the presence of mind to know what possesses you, you're had! You've signed on the line before you know anything about anything.

If you know what possesses you, then maybe you can stop for a minute, take a deep breath, and actually think about the thing with your intelligence. In most cases you'll find that you do have the ability to say no, not because you're a super-yogi or yogini, but because you've actually understood that the drive to throw yourself into a completely absurd circumstance comes from what possesses you, not from a gift of the path, or something that might be interesting.

There are so many facets to self-observation; so many positive consequences, and no negative ones. And this is one of them – to watch yourself in interactions and to know what possesses you. Suppose you see your name on a poster in the local health food store, because you are offering channeling sessions. Even if one person (or nobody) shows up for the session, still, every time you walk in the door, you look at *your* poster, and you feel good because it's a poster with *your* name on it ... on the bulletin board ... in the health food store! And it almost doesn't matter if anybody even comes to the sessions. That poster alone has fulfilled your need to be recognized and acknowledged; to be famous! Even with the slightest bit of power people act like they are running for the president of the United States.

If we learn what possesses us, then we can stop from making asses of ourselves, particularly in circumstances that might cost us our entire life's savings. (It is not only old people who are always being implicated in various scams: somebody promises them this or that, and they take out all their life's savings.)

What possesses us can be little things, but these things still possess us, and they require a tremendous amount of energy to repress, or to contain, or to live out/act out. Sometimes we live out what possess us, like people who go to "open mike nights," always hoping they are going to be discovered.

Karma, Possession and Choice

When you know what possesses you, that knowing gives you a different level of choice. Relative to karma, Dr. Robert

Svoboda[25] says that there are several types of phenomena: some things can be completely avoided; some things can be minimized; and some things are written in stone – they could be put off for another lifetime, but there is no way around them; sooner or later there is a certain manifestation that *is* going to happen. With all the other things, you can work with them. And in many cases, you can work with them to the point where the consequences are so minimized that there is barely an irritation.

The more we know about ourselves, the more we can deal with the kinds of things that *don't need to happen* at all, and with the kinds of things that we are moving toward, having a strong energy toward, but which can be completely minimized or softened. The more we know, the more we can deal with those two categories of karma, which are the vast amount of karma. And, if we know that there is something that we *can't* avoid, by knowing that we can't avoid it, we can at least psyche ourselves up to meet it.

Many things are relatively fated, like your stars. They can be worked with; you can take advantage of them. If you have a tendency in your chart toward music or art, or toward earning money, or guiding others, or politics or teaching or healing ... whatever it might be ... you can optimize that by going into that field professionally. Or, if there are negative aspects of the chart you can often mediate them, modulate them.

The more we know, the more we can meet our karmas with a sense of choice. And when we *know* that what possesses us is not our karmas, or our genetics, but just society,

---

25 Dr. Robert Svoboda is a contemporary author, teacher, Auyervedic astrologer and physician. He is a disciple of the late Swami Vimalananda, an Aghori master. Dr. Svoboda has written extensively on the subject of karma.

culture, advertising, our childhood education, something our third grade teacher said that went in and literally formed our lives, then we can have a greater sense of choice.

Whatever it is that we are carrying with us, if something possesses us that is really pure psychology or personality, those things can be traced down, and we can absolutely eliminate the consequences and the effects of that ruling authority. We can literally relegate that ruling authority to a completely historical domain in our lives. And, when we can have a sense of what rules us karmically, genetically ... we can meet those things with greater clarity.

Possessed by Genetics

This subject of genetic inheritance is a gigantic issue for many people. What if there is a tendency in your family, on the women's side of the family, for ovarian cancer – your mother had it, your grandmother had it, and your mother's sister had it. What if you live your life possessed by that entity? It could be anything – schizophrenia ... there's a big one. People are terrified they are going to go mad. That's gigantic in our culture, hereditary madness!

We may find out that we are possessed by something that we actually do have some genetic tendency toward; it's actually a chemical thing, not our imagination. We have the history of our family to look upon. Still, we can meet that circumstance through diet, through exercise, through right thinking, in a different way than we would meet that thing if we were just riddled with fear and ignorance about the circumstance. You can work with your body and prepare yourself, to optimize or minimize the possibility of the body entering into the same natural genetic condition.

When we used to deal with the subject of subliminal advertising, I used to teach that if you know that subliminals are beings used, those subliminals will not affect you. So, every time you looked at a particular liquor advertisement, but you knew that the picture was full of subliminals – skulls, and sex, and things to create an association in your unconscious mind so you would buy that liquor – they would not affect you. You will have warned your unconscious.

The more we are able to self-observe, and the more we are able to have a sense of what possesses us, the more we will have choice relative to that, even when it is a karmic or a genetic thing.

Possessed by Everything

It is easy to talk about being possessed by something; easy to see the logic in it, and easy to agree with that logic. But, agreeing with the validity of the principle does not mean "knowing" that you are possessed. In order to deal with the things that possess us, we really have to know that we are possessed, not just "agree" with the principle that is a truism. We have to actually enter into a relationship with what possesses us, and in a way that's completely cognizant of the fact that we are either possessed or not; that we either have choice or no choice, but not *some* choice. And how many people want to enter into that realization?

It is pretty easy to come to terms with a physical addiction and to know that it really possesses us. Knowing about possession is a Pandora's box, however. Once you open the understanding of this concept of "being possessed by" something you start realizing that everything we do is a function of some kind of possession. And that is a terrifying realization. We want to think, "Well, I picked up *some* things from my parents, some habits, and sure I really want to be famous, but mostly I'm pretty much in charge." Nope! The realization is, we are *entirely* possessed by various things until we start extricating ourselves, one thing at a time, from that possession.

There are dozens of things we are possessed by that are very easy to extricate ourselves from, because although we are possessed by them, as soon as we realize that possession we realize the absurdity of the logic of those things, and we are literally out of them, above them and beyond their control instantly. But, there are other levels of possession. Possession deepens and deepens. Take something as deep as role-modeling our parents – we all role-model our parents. That is deep! Luckily we role-model all the good things also, not just the bad things, but we role-model our parents, and Joseph Chilton Pearce said that children will become what they *see*, and what the parents expect of them, not what they are told.[26]

Role modeling came from before birth; from the mother – the infant was hooked to her chemistry. So to say, "this possesses me," is true, and yet to know without qualification or doubt the nature of this possession is the nature of workability.

Obviously, then, the question is, "How can we get from recognizing it to knowing it?" First we have to spot it and acknowledge it. That is, in one sense, what "assertion" is. In Arnaud Desjardins' work, they say "accept what is as it is here and now." If "what is as it is here and now" is that we are possessed by anger, and mostly we can keep it under control, but every once in awhile it flares up and we're just

---

26 A renowned author and educator, Joseph Chilton Pearce is the author of *The Magical Child* (N.Y.: Plume, 1992), among many other books.

taken over, to acknowledge the reality of *that*, without judgment or struggle, or the attempt to overpower that thing, is to initiate in the being, in consciousness, that which is capable of extricating ourselves from that possession.

First, list it: "Okay, I'm possessed by this parental influence." Then, every time you notice, from the subtle to gross, any aspect of your physical manifestation, your movement, your emotions or your thought, that you realize comes from your mother or father, you immediately acknowledge that identification or possession. You can acknowledge it by saying, "Oh my God, this is one of the things I'm possessed by." And when we do that enough, our acknowledgement will generate whatever it is – mind, soul, spirit, who knows, or the blessings of the lineage, or grace. The acknowledgement of that state of being, *as it is*, will generate whatever force is necessary to change it, if "change" means moving in a healthy direction, which in the case of parental influence it obviously is.

Workaholic Possession

A participant in Lee's seminar spoke about being obsessed with work – the equivalent of being possessed by an entity, as Lee addressed this subject above. The man was completely overwhelmed with his work, unable to extricate himself from the obsession, and feeling that he could never do enough, or never give enough. He wanted to leave his job, but couldn't.

Lee suggested, first, that he work with finding the source of the obsession, and also suggested that he work on this issue as if it were a theatre project. The application of this approach is usable in many other forms of "possession."

Lee [*addressing the participant*]: You're not sleeping, and you're working around the clock! Where could you possibly get the impression that you are not doing enough or giving enough? Which might be a question you want to pursue: "I'm working to the extent of my energy and capability. Where does this idea come from that I'm not working enough?"

If some simplistic answer comes like, "I'm still trying to please my father; to earn his respect," or something obvious, don't stop there and assume that you've gotten the answer, because that is too superficial. Instead, every time you get the thought, the feeling, that you were describing – the feeling that you can't stop, and that this thing is driving you – allow that emotion to remind you of the question: "Where is this coming from? Where do I get these ideas from?"

If you are working as hard as you are working, then there has to be an inability to draw boundaries for yourself. And, as you're working with that, you might consider looking at the whole thing as a theatre project. When one gets on stage one understands that one is playing a role, and that when that role is finished, one gets offstage and goes back to one's ordinary life.

When you get a project, a job to work on, and you get up in the morning, you do what you need to do, but do it as if you are an actor going to the theatre. There, you spend a full day working on the piece, and then, at the end of the day, you leave the theatre and go home. And, as with many actors and actresses who are passionate about their craft, while at home you may have a conversation about what you're working on, you don't bring the work home!

In America we say, leave your work at the office. Otherwise, because many people are workaholics, they just can't leave their work at the office, especially in the age of personal computers and Internet. All your need is an outlet to plug into, so you don't even need to stay at the office.

Try to discover, without digging and digging, in a relaxed and natural way, what is creating this drive. You do that by observing yourself, and in the observation figuring out where this unnatural relationship to work has come from. And, you don't want to bring the same obsession to the new thing. You don't have to "deal with" your current profession, because it doesn't sound like the problem is with the profession; it sounds like the problem is with you. As we say in English, "Wherever you go, there you are." If you're going to change professions, to go into something new, you don't want to ruin that new job with the same hell.

The outer mind thinks that if we go into a circumstance that has less pressure, and a whole different kind of situation, we'll be able to relax and it will be different. But, it won't be different unless *we're* different. So, you don't want to start the new situation before you've got a little bit of insight into yourself. You need to deal with yourself, and when you're ready to deal with your profession, all you need to do is to fulfill your responsibilities to your clients, and then leave it. Nothing else. You don't need to have some kind of closure about the profession. Simply complete the work you're committed to, and … *finished!*

A lot of people have pretty big sabotage mechanisms; meaning, a lot of people take on more work than they really can do because they have a big investment in being in hell, for obvious psychological reasons. So, as you are trying to leave this old job, be clear that part of you really hates the work and wants to do something else, but another part of you wants to stay in the work. This might lead to taking on a big, long-term job that you won't be able to get out of easily. If you're continuing to take new work, at the same time that you're planning to leave your profession and take on something else, make sure that the new work you take on is not so large and so muddy that you can't get out of it when you're ready.

CHAPTER 4

Enquiry and Emptiness

The practice of enquiry is about finding the source of illusion. The form of enquiry that I recommend in my school is "Who am I kidding?" which could be phrased very loosely as, "Who is it that is under illusion?" The one who is under illusion is the same one who awakens – that is, the same one who is already awake, but functions as if asleep because of being under illusion.

If we remove the illusion, we find ourselves to be awake. We don't have to *do* anything to be awake, because we are already awake, but acting as if we are asleep only because of the illusions.

The "who" and the "I" in "Who am I kidding?" are the same one. The technique of enquiry is about finding that one, that "I." The "I" is actually kidding itself, because in the ultimate scheme of things there is only "One" who acts *as if* there are separate and distinct "ones," but there aren't. There is only One – the "I" is kidding itself.

But then, we don't have to *do* the technique to realize that intellectually. Any intelligent person can come to that conclusion without *doing* anything except thinking about it for a few minutes. However, when this technique is given to you, and when you are instructed by a teacher in its use, it's like empowering a machine by giving it an operator … giving it guidance. It's like the difference between turning on a car, putting it in gear and just letting it go with no driver, or actually driving the car. As is obvious in that metaphor or analogy – or whatever it is: a syllogy? a syllogism? or, who knows *what* those things are (I never did well in grammar, English or French) – if the car is being driven, it is being taken care of, and there is guidance. If the car is not being driven, then it could just bang into a tree or another car.

To do enquiry as empowered by a teacher is to move the understanding of the end result from language to feeling. First you go from knowing the answer intellectually, to getting the answer emotionally, to feeling the answer. And below feeling is infinity. Is that clear? *Never mind.* The real teaching is never through language. Language is like a meat tenderizer. It softens up the system so the real teaching gets to you.

It's not that enquiry can't be valuable or that it can't stimulate the arising of various phenomena if you do it without a master. The danger is (not a big danger, however) that you can draw conclusions that are illusory conclusions, based on what doing the process causes to arise in you. You can take actions or even develop an ongoing habit based on drawing the wrong conclusions.

The reason that it is not terribly dangerous is that we are already full of habits based on drawing conclusions that are illusory. So, what harm in one more illusion? At the same time, the nature of the danger is that in people's minds this technology seems to come from a source that is reliable – a spiritual master. Whatever results they get from using the technique, they tend to be much more attached to than ordinary habits.

Enquire About Everything!

Who we are, *as we are*, is our gateway to practice. It doesn't do any good to wish we were someone else. But, at the same time, everything that arises falls into the same category, which is "not who we are." Everything – happiness, joy, delight, awe, as well as sorrow, guilt, shame, greed, vindictiveness, violence, aggression. The things that are pleasant we like and we want to keep; and the things that are unpleasant we don't like and we want to get rid of.

When we try to practice enquiry, therefore, what we usually do is that, when something uncomfortable arises, something we don't like, we say, "Who am I?" because we want to pierce that discomfort. But, when something that we like arises, we don't question it, because we don't want to pierce it. It's pleasant. The thing about enquiry is, you have to question everything, across the board, without distinction and without discrimination. Otherwise you get a biased view. Otherwise, the one who is questioning is the same one who is maintaining the illusion. And at some point the question has to come from source, from consciousness, not from mind, from ego. But in the beginning, it is only ego. That's what we've got to work with; so we start with ego.

Carlos Castaneda said that Don Juan told him that nobody would enter the path of warriorship if they knew what it was going to cost. People had to be tricked into it. How did Don Juan trick Carlos Castaneda onto the path of warriorship? *Drugs.*

Carlos Castaneda was an anthropologist, and he imagined himself writing a book about the use of peyote among the indigenous tribes of northern Mexico; a book that would make him rich and famous. He didn't want to step onto a path. He didn't want to be a warrior. He just wanted to do some research, write a great book, become rich and famous, and get laid a lot. But Don Juan was not your ordinary peyote-taking Indian. So, Castaneda began to work with

Don Juan. There was lots of peyote, but after a while, a year or two, the peyote stopped. That's when Castaneda said, "Hey how come you're not giving me peyote anymore. Aren't we doing to do more research?" And Don Juan said, "Oh no, we don't need that anymore. That's child's play. That was just to get you hooked. Now we're going to get to the real stuff."

Enquiry is about questioning everything. It always starts with ego. Ego starts asking, "Who am I? Who am I?" And if you're really serious about discovering the answer to that question, pretty soon you figure out that it's not working, and you wonder *why is it not working?* Then you figure out that it's not working because ego is doing it. And then you say, "Well, how can I do it a different way so that it's effective?" That's the beginning of being able to access levels of consciousness that are not dominated by the authoritarian autonomy of the ego.

When you discover what's not working, it gives you a lot more fuel toward discovering what does work. In traditional Advaita Vedanta practice, one of the forms of practice is to negate everything.[27] They call it *neti, neti,* which means "not this, not this." With everything you perceive you say, "Not this." Because the underlying question is "What is real?" or "What is true?" So, everything you think, everything you emote, everything you feel, you notice it and you say, "Not this." Nothing that has definition is real.

On the other hand, everything is real. But you can't start from that realization. You can start assuming that realization, but it doesn't mean that realization will be true of you. First you have to discover that nothing is real, and then

---

27 Advaita Vedanta is the doctrine (based in the Vedic scriptures) of non-dualism taught by Sankaracharya (484 C.E.)

you can begin to relate to the world from the platform that everything is real.

Why did God make things that way? Perversity! And believe it or not, that *is* the answer; nothing more profound than that. However, here we are, and things are, so wishing things were otherwise doesn't make a difference. Wishing that God were ultimately benign and cared personally about each one of us doesn't make it so. Creation is this unending volcanic eruption. It only has one purpose, to keep going ... evolution!

Form and Emptiness

In Buddhism there are two important little phrases. One is, "*samsara* is *nirvana* and *nirvana* is *samsara*," and the other from the *Diamond Sutra* is, "form is emptiness and emptiness is form." One of the things you find out when you investigate yourself is that all phenomena simply arise and subside with no reason and no purpose. And all form, broken down to its primal level, is essentially nothingness. All appearances are insubstantial (physics tells us that). Of course, to *realize* that about yourself, about your mind, your consciousness, your brilliance ... all of that ... can be very shocking. The same with "*samsara* is *nirvana*."

Samsara means "this world," the world of appearances, and *nirvana* means "the world of bliss." "*Samsara* is *nirvana*" is a very freeing realization because you realize that heaven is not elsewhere; it is *right here* and *now*, at this very moment. But, many people get stuck there at the midway point. They realize that "form is emptiness," and the shock of it is so startling that they go into some kind of altered state of consciousness, and they stay there. Some go mad, some imagine themselves to be spiritual teachers, which is a different form of madness, and some simply are so shocked by the realization that they reject the whole aspect of spiritual life entirely and run away from it.

Those who realize that "*samsara* is *nirvana*" are usually so thrilled by the idea that they start acting as if they could do anything that they wanted – because they are in "heaven" – and because there will be no retribution. Or they become spiritual teachers, imagining that they've had this full awakening. It's a very powerful trip.

But, this realization is only fifty percent of the formula. The other part is, "*nirvana* is *samsara*," and "emptiness is form." Most people never get to that because the first realization is so overwhelming and it appears to be so complete, so total, that they don't go further. We must always go further. There is always something more. Always!

We are born, we die, yet there is something more. Even if we get enlightened, there is still something more. If we go into *samadhi*, there is something more ... always something more.

When you realize that "emptiness is form," that is also very shocking. The appearances or forms, which had seemed completely fleeting and ephemeral after the first half of the realization, now all of a sudden become absolute reality. Therefore, in any given moment when you are sad, for instance, you can no longer say that it is an illusion, because it is total and complete and perfect as it is – "emptiness is form."

The full realization manifests in many ways, but one of the ways it manifests is in not making any distinctions or separations anymore, not even about the fact that form is completely and entirely empty.

And "*nirvana* is *samsara*" is a bummer of a realization, because you realize that there is no ultimate heaven and that you can never get away! This ... this life ... this reality ... as it is, is it! Nothing else. Wow, what a drag! I mean, if you're happy and healthy and everything is great then it isn't so bad. If you're kicking around on the lower end of the spectrum, however, it's a different story. You think to yourself, "This is it? It is never going to get any better?"

Of course, every moment is different. So, one moment could be terrible, the next moment could be ecstatic. In fact, the way it usually works is, when you've had such a total and revolutionary revelation, the universe tends to create, in your general area, the arising of phenomena that are quite pleasant. But not always. Ramana Maharshi had cancer, and when he was dying he would nap frequently and moan in his sleep.[28] When he would wake up, his attendants would ask, "Oh Master, were you in pain? Were you suffering?"

He would say, "What suffers? Who suffers?" And "Who suffers?" is the same as "Who am I kidding?"

That is what we are struggling to find out.

Rely on Emptiness

Emptiness – that's the truth of things!

The more you open, the "bigger" the emptiness becomes. And if you were able to open totally, you would find endless and abiding emptiness, because that's all there is. Everything else is an illusion. There is nothing but emptiness, covered by the appearance of things that spontaneously arise and subside without any actual relationship to the reality of everything – which is emptiness.

---

28 Ramana Maharshi (1879-1950) was a Tamil Hindu Jivanmukta (enlightened master) who realized spiritual liberation at age sixteen. He lived at the base of the sacred mountain, Arunachala, in Tiruvannamalai, South India. His teaching is nonduality, and the form of enquiry he used and shared is the phrase, "Who am I?"

I would suggest going "into" the emptiness, rather than looking for some kind of unitive experience to obscure the emptiness. The emptiness is the truth. Everything else is illusion, and the mind finds that reprehensible. The mind wants all of "this" – this illusion – to have substance; to be real; to be safe and secure. The mind wants all of this to be abiding and reliable. But it's not.

The actual beingness of everything is emptiness. There is nothing to hold onto. The floor *is* solid, however, and you can stand on the ground of your intelligence and your skills and your life, and all of that. But, if you were to realize the end of the path – enlightenment, awakening, realization, freedom, whatever it is – then the floor, the ceiling, the walls would all fall away, and there would be nothing but emptiness. It's very reliable.

So, go into the emptiness, no matter how much fear may arise as you enter into that process. The ego will fight with every weapon at its disposal – with depression, frustration, doubt, everything. But, leave nothing behind. Don't even keep a little.

* * *

Questioner: *The object of my love has withdrawn from me, and I keep hoping that I can turn that love to Love for the Beloved, but I'm still having a hard time letting go of the personal attachment.*

Lee: You establish your intention correctly, which is to *see through* the object of your love, which is form, and ultimately empty. When you're able to see through *that*, what you find is the Divine on the other side. But, that doesn't happen in a week or a month necessarily, at least not stably, but you may experience moments of it.

Once your intention is properly defined, keep re-establishing it. There is no mechanistic formula for how to do that, you just keep re-establishing intention, and keep saying (in your own words), "I need this to fall on the Divine as my object of Love." Keep establishing *that* ... and it will happen when it happens.

Coincidently, the struggles with disconnecting from the personal are all in the psychological domain, and you work on that as you would work on any psychological circumstance: self-observation and consideration, and disentangling the knots that keep psychological habits in place. So, this "unhooking" is one thing, but the transfer of your attention is in a whole different domain from the psychological. For that, you establish intention and you keep asking for it.

Questioner: *Does working in the psychological domain have any bearing on the other domain?*
Lee: Of course. If all the attention that's wrapped up in the knot is freed up, then of course that's going to have an effect, a positive effect. These domains are not the same but they're tied in together.

CHAPTER 5

Neurotic Mind and Work Mind

The following lengthy excerpt first appeared in the book As It Is, A Year on the Road with A Tantric Teacher, by M. Young (Prescott, Arizona: Hohm Press, 1999). The book records scores of talks and exchanges Lee had with students and guests over the course of one year, 1999. Because of its relevance to this subject of mind and emotions, the distinction Lee made about "neurotic mind / Work mind" is reprinted here.

Lee: [Carlos] Castaneda wrote about Don Juan's description of the fact that we have two different minds. Carlos said that he thought for years that Don Juan said, "There are two parts of our mind." And then he realized that Don Juan said, "We have two different minds. And you have to drop one mind and live in the other mind." Carlos kept trying to deal with two aspects of mind and he said he never could, he was just totally unsuccessful at realizing anything that Don Juan was saying. Finally when he realized that Don Juan said we have two minds instead of two parts of the mind, then he began to really progress.

That can be a useful way of looking at things. We have what we could call the family dynamic with all its neurotic implications, the mind of the child having made certain decisions about his or her world or about reality based on a child's intelligence, a child's understanding, a child's expectations and projections. That mind grows up to be, as we all know, absolutely consuming. That mind possesses us. We identify with it as if that mind were us. Sooner or later in this Work we've got to break with that mind, cleanly and finally. We have to break with that mind and everything it stands for – all its elements, all its identifications, its hopes, its dreams, its wishes, and its morality. Each of us has that mind to some degree in terms of our political leanings. Even when we say, "Oh it's terrible, only a week ago there was supposed to be a cease-fire, but the Serbs just went into some Albanian village and shot down a bunch of people." We all have our social and political sense of things and often that sense is humanistic, it's very magnanimous, very generous, and maybe even compassionate. But every single element of that mind has to be severed. We have to literally stop functioning out of the context of that mind.

Then there is the other mind, which is the mind that sees reality *as it is* – without projections and expectations and subjectivity. That is the mind that sees reality simply as it is, moment to moment. That mind certainly has its full complement of feeling – outrage at social injustices and so on – but that mind has an entirely different context than the mind of our original survival strategy. This Work could be said to be a matter of moving beyond the first mind and coming to be rooted and residing in the second mind, which is the mind of objective reality, the mind of clarity, the mind of truth, the mind of the Divine. This is the dilemma we all face in one form or another … .

The secret to dealing with the demand of this Work is being able to recognize, in any given situation, what the space or circumstance is calling for — objectively, of course. The demand may simply be to be in meditation every morning at seven o'clock, or just to cook a dinner that everybody on the ashram or in the household will find wholesome and nutritious. It could be anything from moment to moment. The demand could be to be a space of safety and sanctuary for one's partner … .

So there's always a Work demand, whether it's simply at an ordinary personal level in a task that's been given, or something else. The Work is about recognizing which of the two minds is dominating our consciousness in every moment. Over time the aim is to minimize the first mind, the neurotic mind, and maximize the second mind–the mind of unity, clarity, truth.

The Work will chip away, chip away, chip away at the first mind, but at some point for most of us we will get thrown into really deep considerations in which there are only two options. The options are so intense that we're forced into looking at them clearly and recognizing the degree to which the neurotic mind dominates and controls us. There are always only two options, and they're always the options of the neurotic mind or we could say, the awakened mind, the Work mind. Actually that's a good phrase for it. There is the neurotic mind and the Work mind; those are always the only two options.

The Work often puts us in a situation in which we are forced to look at the degree to which we are not free, in which we have no choice based on the control of the first mind. And then we have to ask ourselves, do we want to be free? Do we want the option that is freedom? The answer is always yes, and then that option becomes clear. But, to choose the option of the Work mind, we have to be willing to step away from the claws of and out of the jaws of the neurotic mind. That is a very difficult thing to do because there is no comfort in the Work mind. None whatsoever. There's no comfort in the Work mind because we can't ever choose to seek the kinds of comfort that deny the Work if we step beyond the neurotic mind. All the neurotic mind does is buffer us against reality, against truth. So to actually make that choice, the intensity of the demand on either side has to be great enough that we see what it is we're up to. We see what the choice is. When the intensity is such that you cannot deny the death of the neurotic mind and the life and freedom of the Work mind, then you are in a position in which you can make a step.

Often we make a choice that's good for our work out of some moral idea, but we don't really *feel* it. And in not really feeling, we aren't seeing. We don't see the nature of mind. We may make the right choice but we're just making it out of obligation, or even out of love for the teacher, which is wonderful. But we're still not seeing. When we're thrown into a position where the intensity of the choice is so great that the suffering of the neurotic mind is overwhelming, then we're drowning in the pain of it and we are forced to make a choice. The choice of freedom forces us to see the elements of the neurotic mind and the free mind. We're forced to see how absolutely, completely choiceless we are when we are dominated by our psychology, and the shock of that is what propels us into choosing the Work mind.

One of the reasons we aren't always choosing practice is because we think we have choice. Yes, we're neurotic. Everybody's neurotic, but unconsciously we actually believe that we have choice about anything – to stop smoking, or to start smoking without becoming addicted again, or this, that, or the other thing. We really do not recognize the fact that we have no choice. We are totally enslaved by the neurotic mind: every breath, every word out of our mouths, every gesture. We couldn't be free if our lives, if our children's lives, depended upon it. We *could* not. We have no options – we can't be free. We can't make the conscious choice. We can't make a free gesture. When we get that, the horror and disgust is so overwhelming that we will be forced to choose the Work mind. But we will never see it with that clarity if we aren't thrown into circumstances that are way over our heads, that create an intensity, a crisis within us which produces that kind of vision.

E.J. Gold once answered the question, "How did you find the Work?" saying, "I had nothing left to live for." That's how dramatic the circumstances have to be to make us choose the Work consciously. Many of us at times make statements like, "I can't leave the Work." Okay, that may be true, but there are still many moments in which we do not choose the Work, in which we're lazy. We want to live because we have this idea that the future holds something for us: love and fulfillment and satisfaction, peace and blah, blah, blah. But as we are it's literally impossible to realize anything that we hope for from the teacher, from the path, or from life itself. E.J. Gold realized that he had nothing left to live for, and at that moment he chose the Work. When you have that kind of a realization, when you choose the Work, you can't afford one minute of laziness. You cannot afford to be toxified. You cannot afford to close your eyes. You cannot afford to relax your vigilance. You cannot afford to buffer yourself from the Work, even for a moment of comfort.

Ultimately this Work is designed to throw every single one of us into a crisis so deep and so profound, so mind-shattering, that we never recover. This is the realization that we come to: that as we are, as mechanical beings, freedom is a literal impossibility. There is only one option and it's the Work, and the Work does not wait around. The Work moves and if we can move with it, it will honor us and it will feed us and it will care for us. If we are not willing to move with it, it will crush us under its heel, with no remorse and no sentimentality.

Sooner or later, every one of us will be thrown into such a conflict. That conflict is designed to produce freedom, and we may get thrown into it many times, because we don't get it. The first time we make a little shift, and the second time another little shift. Yes, the sangha bonds more deeply, and we come to love one another. We come to love our partner more than our own lives, we love our children more than our own lives. We find ourselves sometimes in situations in which the things we have always looked for in life – the heart of longing, and sweetness and tenderness and affection – are all there, but all of that is just icing on the cake. This Work is not designed to produce worldly satisfaction – love, tenderness, devotion. It's designed to produce freedom, and in freedom we can love one another profoundly, sacredly, deeply.

We can be catapulted into transcendental states that can last for months simply by a look between one another. But those are the *affects* of freedom, those are not the intention of the Work. The intention of the Work is to produce freedom in us. There's only one way that freedom can be produced in us and that is to choose Work mind over neurotic mind. It has to be a conscious choice, and the only way that we'll ever make a choice that's conscious, fully conscious, is to see neurotic mind in its totality, in its death. To see it for what it is – empty of all substance, empty of all possibility, empty of all creativity, empty of all genuine, human feeling, empty of heart, empty of mind, empty of everything except its own mechanical survival impetus. That's it. Until we see it that way, until we see our lives, our love for our parents, our drive for sexual fulfillment, our taste for fine food, our love of good music – until we see all of it as nothing, absolutely *nothing* but totally mechanical, dead slavery to neurotic mind – we'll never choose the Work in a way that allows us to consciously be the kind of warrior that Castaneda is describing.[29]

* * *

Choosing Work Mind

The following question was asked to Lee in December 2001:

Questioner: *How does one choose Work mind over neurotic mind?*

Lee: Sometimes our clarity is so great that the Work Mind is obvious. Then we are carried by that clarity. When neurotic mind reasserts itself, we are called to remember how clear the choice for Work was. We have to remember and act on that, despite the resistance, until we break the habit of neurotic mind. Then, at some point, Work Mind predominates and it becomes easier to stay there. That can take a few seconds, or lifetimes, because some people just have a larger mass to deal with. Keep establishing intention, keep pushing forward. But don't get caught in dramatizing failure. Work Mind is what serves evolution over and against one's survival mechanism.

29 Young, M. *As It Is: A Year on the Road with a Tantric Teaching*. Prescott, Arizona: Hohm Press, 2000, pp. 154-157.

CHAPTER 6

Conceptual Thinking and the Grasping Mind

Bob Dylan said, "To live outside the law, you must be honest." Wow! Every time I hear that there's a moment of bliss. I tend to like phrases that seem paradoxical, and I don't try to understand them. The thing is, paradox is a fixation of mind. In reality, in the Universe, there is no such thing as paradox.

The music critic for the *N.Y. Times* said about Bob Dylan that none of his albums are as good as one of the songs on the album, and none of the songs is as good as one line in the song. And Bob Dylan knows this. I've worshipped him for forty years; and I don't understand why. It took me forty years to come up with the obvious way that Bob Dylan works, which is, "Good enough is good enough." Bob Dylan is a genius. He knows what the *N.Y. Times* critic says is true. But he's busy being an artist, and he can't waste time making sure that every line is as good as those perfect lines.

When something – like this statement of Dylan's – really stops someone for a minute, we say it "boggles" the mind. Every time that happens, it's useful. Because, it gives us a break, even if only for an instant, from the absolute grip our mechanicality has over us. And even if we don't reflect on it that way, every time we're stopped for a second, for an instant, something very valuable happens – we have an instant of reality, even if we don't know it. We're not conscious of it at all. But the body knows it.

Camille Paglia – another one of my contemporary heroines, a fantastic writer, and thinker and human being – is a teacher in a university, and she teaches a course on Bob Dylan. She says that when great artists create, most of the time they don't even know what they're doing. They know they're creating great art, but the details are unimportant. And she said, "If Bob Dylan came and sat in one of my classes and heard the way I was interpreting his language he'd say, 'That's crazy. I wasn't thinking about that when I wrote that song. I just wrote the song.'" Yet somehow, through some quirk of fate, an artist, a musician, a painter, a sculptor, a dancer, a martial artist produces something that comes from somewhere else, and let's say – to avoid confusion for those of you who might think I mean from space people – that they come from the Absolute. And those things, whatever they are, have a certain glimmer.

Being Touched

When we have an organic response to something, often, being thinking creatures, we have this pernicious need to understand everything rationally. Sometimes people will come into the room of the Sacred Bazaar,[30] or walk onto the property of Hauteville, and start crying. It's a little embarrassing, and sometimes they say to themselves, "What's going on? What's happening?"

---

30 *Sacred Bazaar* is the name Lee has given to the vast array of sacred art and artifacts that he has collected for many years, and which he displays and sells at various programs and seminars wherever he travels throughout the world.

When we respond on an organic level to teachings, to other people, to objects of beauty, to music, we may not have a linear or a rational way to explain the intensity of our response. Even if we are feeling *something* – maybe its music – many times we listen and we go, "That's crazy, I must just be making this up." But if we give our response credibility, we will always reap the benefits of that influence that we have become accessible to.

People also tell me about their dreams. They say, "I had this dream. I don't know what it means. It's a little disturbing. Can you help me understand it?" If I feel the dream is a positive indication, my response is, "It *feels like* a good dream to me. You don't need to question it. You don't need to understand it. The influence is positive. Just accept it. And just let its influence work, and don't worry about the details." Although somebody said, "God is in the details," which is also true ... but in a different context.

For me, the response is enough. Being touched is the thing! I don't care about all of the intellectual components, the rational components surrounding that. I just want to be touched. If I'm touched, I'm happy. I don't need to know where it comes from, and why and what it means, and where it's going, because our being is ultimately intelligent, and will use whatever is useful.

So, that's what I trust – being touched! And if my mind goes along and understands, great, that's sort of extra. But if it doesn't, it doesn't matter so much, because the being is going to capitalize on whatever food is offered it that is nutritious.

Non-Conceptual Mind

One of the ways we find ourselves in the non-conceptual is to recognize when we are in the conceptual – i.e., when we are imprisoned by our conventional thinking – which is, basically, all the time. This "mind" is so habitual that we don't recognize it and define it as that. We just accept it, without thinking, without consideration, without investigation. What the Vajrayana teaching recommends[31] – besides an extreme practice of prayer, which includes prostration, mantra and *puja* – is a profound investigation of our ordinary behavior as a way to distinguish the non-conceptual dharma from our ordinary behavior.[32]

Our ordinary behavior is bound, completely, by conceptual thinking. As one of my students noted recently, she saw that, in the worse conflicts she had with people, there was no way out except to take a leap. She remembered what I had been saying for years – that it doesn't matter who is right and who is wrong. She remembered to ask herself, "Do you want to be right or do you want to be free of that hell realm?" Because, she said, "Being right is just another hell realm, and nothing creative can come out of that."

Namkhai Norbu[33] says that Vajrayana Buddhism is designed to give you practices that are realistic for an ordinary human being. In other words, you can't start in the Buddha realm; you have to start where you are. If you practice with enough diligence, then your relationship to the conceptual dharma

---

31 Lee had been reading to his students from the book *Dakini's Warm Breath: The Feminine Principle in Tibetan Buddhism* by Judith Simmer-Brown (Boston, Mass.: Shambhala Publishers, 2002).

32 A conceptual dharma (doctrines or teachings) can be studied in books, and can be discussed and questioned with our teachers, and with other members of the sangha. There is also a huge "non-conceptual" dharma which is not so easy to pin down. For students and devotees in the tradition in which Lee teaches it may include our inner experiences of devotion in the master's presence, the content of our dreams, our observations of the way in which the master moves or speaks to us, to the ways in which we find ourselves being spontaneously moved by forces seemingly beyond our control.

33 Chögyal Namkhai Norbu is the founder and guide of the Dzogchen Community, a Tibetan Buddhist foundation. He has lived in the West since 1960 and is the author of many books.

becomes more and more refined, until it becomes so refined that it is ungraspable, and then you're really getting someplace. Those are the higher levels of practice.

What allows you to "be in the world but not of the world" is your willingness to consider the dharma as the primacy of what you do with your mind, rather than all the movies, movie stars, sports figures, or even art that you are attracted to, or the pornographic novels that you love to read, or everything else that you usually do with your mind. What this means is that you are willing to love the dharma, and study it, and talk about it and live it and practice it. Your life becomes a satellite to the life of the path, in whatever kind of gravity the path has with you. The dharma really grabs you!

Dharma Dharma Dharma

The only way to refine the conceptual, to the point where it becomes so refined that you can't quite grasp it, is through consideration of the dharma, which is why in Buddhism there is such a tremendous emphasis on dharma, dharma, dharma. There is so much study, so much debate, because that is how you refine the conceptual. You don't refine the conceptual through philosophy. You refine the conceptual through refining the conceptual, only.

Practice gives you the foundation and the discipline to be able to continue to keep your wits about you, to stay focused on the dharma, basically, instead of falling into the hell realm of reading biographies of Kobe Bryant[34] or Mike Tyson,[35] as fascinating as they might be.

---

34 Kobe Bryant, contemporary highly-paid star in the U.S. NBA (National Basketball Association), noted for his extreme behavior.
35 Mike Tyson, former heavyweight boxing champion of the world.

People tell me that they often engage that kind of material with the rationalization that they can extract some kind of work value from it. And, there is truth in that, as long as they aren't hooked by the fascination with it. As soon as we have the thought, referring to Kobe Bryant, such as, "Well, of course when you give a twenty-year-old all that power and money ..." we've completely lost any conceivable relationship to the subject matter as something that might have work value.

If you listen to most discussions of art, like the ones they have in movies, which I guess are designed to be satirical in some sense, there is such intellectual game playing going on, that even when the concepts themselves might open a window onto something useful, the mind/the intellect completely locks the possibility out of it. We get completely enamored by the height of our intellectual consideration.

Obviously, one of the dangers of practicing a tantric path[36] without having some degree of stability on the foundational paths is that, while you have a sense of the possibility that lies within any experience, any conversation, any mood, you don't have the refinement to recognize how desires and attachments completely mask the possibility of actually using those doorways.

So, you make a statement like, "This is tantric work, so any experience is useful." Well, yes, that's an essential truth, but we don't know that any experience is useful. We haven't defined for ourselves how completely we are in the grip of the lower mind and emotion. Until we define *that*, and really come to workable terms with it, we can't possibly practice tantra.

---

36 tantric path, an advanced form of practice characterized by the non-rejection of all things; not to be confused with the limited popular understanding of tantra as sexual yoga.

The Grasping Mind

To come to workable terms with this understanding of our mind means that, as our life provides us with opportunities, we notice our own grasping – whether that grasping be for territory, or for company, or for no company, or for privacy, for solitude, or for money, or for material things, or comfort, or even organic vs. non-organic food. It could be something very healthy. But any grasping undermines our work. If we don't realize how we are grasping, we can't possibly practice tantra.

Ordinarily, in our flow through life, we have a tremendous number of opportunities every day to recognize grasping. For example, one day we were standing in the office and a police car came driving down the hill, on our property. Somebody said, "There's a police car on the property!" I looked out, and there it was, with its lights blinking, and I just assumed that the police were looking for a house and didn't know the territory and went up the wrong driveway. But, anyone who noticed that police car could take a look at the shock in their body and note the reaction in their mind: "There is a police car, on *our* property." We become personally implicated. We think, "What are *they* here for?" The first thing we think of is, "They're raiding the cult." (That's the first thing *I* think of, not the first thing "we" think of. I'm not so innocent.)

We need to look at our grasping to be left alone; our grasping for security, for sanctuary, for safety in the most mundane ways, not even in the spiritual sense, but just personally. We need to note that rush of energy that goes up the spine when we see a police car on the property, or *whatever it is*! Like hearing burning dogs howling.[37] And then, hearing the shot. On one hand being relieved that the dog is dead. But on the other hand thinking, "That guy shot his own dog."

We need to look at our grasping with regard to the whole relationship to guns ... to shooting a pet that we love ... to whatever it might be. Even in a moment of relief there is still an opportunity to see what the mind does; what we grasp at. Not to mention what we grasp at in a tough financial situation, or a tough health situation, or a tough sexual situation.

I don't know how it is for other people in the area of sex, and I don't have all that much experience in general, anyway. But, as an insecure man, my experience is that it doesn't matter how many times sex "works." It doesn't matter how many times it is fabulous. It doesn't matter how many times there is positive feedback (I think this may have happened once in my life where somebody actually said, "Wow, that was great."). There can be five years of fantastic sexual heroism, and one night when something doesn't work (guess what that *something* is?), and all the old fears, all the old insecurities, are right there again. It's like you never had a successful encounter, however one defines *sex*. Just *getting through* the fucking thing is success for me. Just making it to the "other side."

That's the grasping mind! It absolutely does not matter how much feedback, how much success, how much ... whatever, we get. When there is grasping, that grasping will hide itself, and as soon as it has an opportunity, it's out in the open again.

---

37 During a recent fire on the property adjoining Lee's Arizona ashram, some dogs were trapped inside a burning building.

What Fascinates Me?

Practice, practice, practice weakens the muscle of grasping. If you practice with enough diligence, then, the grasping arises but literally has no force. There is no grip. Then you can go on to higher practice.

The way you have to practice is: you have to return your mind to the dharma every time, even if people around you are talking about some famous sports figure, or the Academy Awards, or some movie star. Fine, you don't want to be a wet blanket on every conversation; you don't want to walk into some group and find that everybody turns their back as soon as you sit down in the circle. But, when we find ourselves in a mundane conversation, instead of saying, "Oh, let's discuss Buddha dharma," the thing to do within yourself is to inquire about what part of the conversation dramatizes your grasping. Is it the fact that some basketball player is making twenty-million dollars a year and he's just a kid? Is it the fact that everyplace he goes women swarm all over and want to sleep with him? Is it the fact that he is a precision athletic instrument? Do you want to hear more details about how somebody rose up out of the ghetto, and now have bought their mother and father new homes and new cars? How they're putting all their brothers and sisters through university? *Whatever it is.* Pay attention in the conversation to where and how are you grasping. That's how you make use of it.

Practice means to dig down to the root of our motive for enjoying the conversation, if the conversation is beyond just simple social engagement, which it usually is. "Where is my grasping?" That's how you bring your mind back to dharma. You take whatever circumstance you are in, and you return it to dharma: "If I can discover the roots of my grasping, then I have a chance to sever it at the roots, instead of just at the bud." You know that if you clip flowers at the bud, more flowers grow. One stalk, clip the bud, and two stalks grow. Clip both buds, four stalks grow. And before you know it, you have a lot of flowers out of a one flower plant.

If we clip our desires at the bud, all we have is more desires. If we get to the root, then we have a chance to enter into a more substantial practice. That's how we turn everything into dharma. We investigate our own inner landscape relative to dharma.

We don't have to throw in Buddhist concepts or Sanskrit words. In the simplest of terms we are educated to turn to what is going on in any given moment; we turn to, "What am I actually doing now? Where am I grasping? What are my emotional hooks? What's my motive? What's my payoff?" When that's what we look at within ourselves, we don't need to share our brilliant insights with everybody in the group. We let the conversation go on, and *we* bring our minds to the refuge of dharma. But that requires tremendous disciplining. Why? Because we are so easily distracted, and so easily fascinated; completely lost in the world of our attachments. So, we ask ourselves, what fascinates me about that particular story? Am I living vicariously? Is that *my* dream of fame?

Talking about a dream of fame ... look at David Bowie, for instance, who several years ago couldn't even get a record contract. *David Bowie!* One of the stellar figures in music in the twentieth century, and he couldn't get a record contract. *Oh, my God!* The other musicians and I can look at that and say, "At least he had his shot, okay. Fine, we're all in the same place: he's looking for a record deal and we're looking for a record deal." Yeah, but he's David Bowie! He's looking for a record deal *after* a stunning career, having realized every conceivable aspect of fame and fortune. And we haven't had our shot, and we're getting a little old for it.

Whoever we are, we ask: What's my personal fascination with any story? Where is the grasping? And we look at the roots of that: What am I *really* looking for? Is it *really* fame I'm after, or is it simply recognition, love, acknowledgement, regard, respect? We have to keep digging to get to the roots of our desire. Because at the very roots of desire, of grasping, also lies the reality of spontaneous interdependent arising.[38]

You keep refining, refining, refining, and you get closer, and closer and closer. And at one point, you're right there. And then you ask, "Oh my God! What in fact *is* reality?" Because you've refined everything down to the point where you realize that all the things you thought were substantial are empty.

Working with the Confused Mind

Questioner: I've been going through chaos on the affective level. Feeling confused.

Lee: What is your profession?

Questioner: Lawyer.

Lee: A lawyer who admits to confusion? I don't believe it.

Questioner: A new page is being turned in relationship to my work; choices to make; and I don't see clearly the situation to make right choices.

Lee: There is this funny phenomena: A lot of my students

---

38 "Spontaneous interdependent arising" is the realization that everything is interdependent; that no person and no event is independent from everything else.

are therapists, and they have all the same problems as their clients, so they bring their problems to me. And they explain the problem, and I say something to the effect that, "If you were a client that brought you this problem, how would you handle it?" And they always know exactly how they would handle the problem with the client, but somehow they are not applying that knowledge to themselves.

If you have difficulty making clear choices, simply treat every choice you have to make as a case, and being a lawyer (he's probably a very sharp lawyer and perceptive), the answer will be obvious, quickly. Try that.

Questioner: There is this subtle boundary, for me, between waiting for something and taking right action. How to decide?

Lee: When the mind is trying to figure that out, then, at best, any decision is going to be an educated guess. Because the mind will have more or less information about the situation, more or less insight into causes and consequences and the whole environment surrounding it.

You may be very successful at educated guesses, and you might make the right choices, just out of being good at making educated guesses. If, however, you want the decisions to be a function of reality, then you have to accept submersion in reality. So, "welcome without taking,"[39] and reality will make the right decision, in the right time in the right place. It might feel like *you* are making the decision, but it is really reality making the decision.

So, it is back to practice.

---

39 "Welcome without taking" is a phrase used by Arnaud Desjardins, reflecting the teaching of his master, Swami Prajnanpad. It refers to a mood in which one is receptive without grasping.

Letting Go

Questioner: I understood through my spiritual teacher that one "lets go" of something when one is mature enough; when one is ready; when it is right.

Lee: Bob Dylan said "Nostalgia is death." There is a difference between nostalgia, which is maintaining the attachment after the thing is over, and having a memory about something that is filled with sweetness and tenderness.

It is true that a mature practitioner, a mature person, is able to let go, but you can't erase your memory, or you wouldn't want to. Letting go has to do, first of all, with the action, and then with holding the new space you are in with maturity and sensitivity.

I remember Arnaud Desjardins talking with me about the first time he went to India. He was a young man with a big camera and a new family – a wife and baby. One day he got in his Land Rover and drove across Europe. He spoke about that trip with such wonder: "What an adventure, what a great thing we did. We were young then." There was a tremendous enjoyment of an experience of the past, but not an ongoing attachment to it.

With Arnaud Desjardins also there was an equal enjoyment of the experience of the present. So, for instance, if you have a house you love and you feel nostalgic about leaving it, you can also be as much in love with the next place you live as you were with this original house. It's not like one replaces the other. That first house will always have its place in your life, in your experience.

The issue is not so much about attachment, it is about holding on to attachment and trying to make it eternal. If you allow the past to be *what it is*, you allow the present to be what it is, and the future will be what it is. Then you can still have attachments to the past and the present. If you hold everything in a context of maturity, you see that you have attachments, but it doesn't override your ability to act rightly.

After all, look how many people are divorced and yet they fall in love again. Somebody who can't let go would get divorced and say, "It's horrible, I'm in so much pain I am never getting married again." They would wall themselves off. They would be cold and harsh and cynical. I mean, that's the way I handled *my* divorce.

Don't make mountains out of molehills. I had a motorcycle I used to drive and I was *very* attached to it. One day I was hit by a car and the motorcycle got all smashed up, finished, worse than me – I survived quite well. I guess we are lucky, people bounce and metal doesn't. Metal gets crushed.

The insurance company said, "We are going to pay you for the bike, but we are going to take the bike away." (These insurance companies aren't going to let you have your bike and ride it too.) My relationship to the motorcycle is exactly the same as the relationship to the old house, or whatever we are attached to. Everybody has those things. That's life! We have our desires, our attachments, our … whatever. So it's not a problem.

Certain forms of love have their period of time. Then they grow and then they end. There is a sweetness to the ending as there is to the sustaining of it. Lots of you probably have an easier time letting go than I do, I think. I'm still waiting for the next motorcycle.

Nobody in my family is waiting, however. They are very grateful.

CHAPTER 7

The Dividing Mind

Our identification with illusion becomes most acute when we separate any aspect of our reality from whatever we think reality is supposed to be. If we think reality is supposed to be nondual, yet we perceive the world around us as being dualistic (and therefore "unreal"), then of course we run into difficulties.

As time has gone on, this Western Baul teaching[40] has moved ultimately toward what is completely human – which is, regardless of whether we subscribe to the notion that the world is a creation of our mind, still, *what is, is.* You know that little philosophical gem from certain of the Indian traditions, that, "There is no world. You make up the world because you have senses and what you see is really illusory"? That's well and good until you get to be sixty and twist your back and can't get out of bed for four days, or if you walk in front of a truck.

Anyway, it's easy to say that all reality is illusion, that all perception is an illusion, until a house burns down. I don't know how any Indian woman who's ever been in labor and had a baby could subscribe to the philosophy that all of our

---

40 The Western Baul teaching is represented by Lee Lozowick. This path originated with the Bauls of Bengal, India, a sixth-century sect founded by Chaitanya. A group of musicians and beggars, who loosely align with the sahajiya path of Buddhism, the tantric Vaisnava tradition, and the path of Sufi mystics, the Bauls are iconoclasts who seek the "man of the heart," the Divine who indwells in each being.

perceptions are illusory and that everything is created by our own mind. It's completely nonsensical. But, a lot of people try to figure things that way.

Enlightened duality, which is the basis of my teaching, is about the realization that *what is, is*. When we separate – through the use of philosophy – we are essentially creating suffering for ourselves. Because the act of separation, itself, is what creates an antagonism between the part of us that is seeking God, union, or whatever ... and the part of us that is human – the part that is perceiving the other, perceiving the world around us, including the leaves falling off the trees in the fall.

As long as we divide, we label things – such as, "This is my personality ... this is my psychology ... this is my essence ... my astral body, causal body, ethereal body." Of course, once we give labels then we relate to those things with certain distinctions. We do that for the sake of conversation, and since we all have to start somewhere, we start from where we are. However, when we see things *without division*, then we can relate to those things from a different perspective.

Changing Perspective

Ordinarily, and particularly in the Gurdjieff work, when the "I's" of personality and psychology dominate our function, we can't "Work" because we are multiple beings. As long as we stay within the perspectives that we are usually locked into – the "I's" we are consistently locked into – the conflict will remain. We may make a decision that is positive and creative, or a decision that makes things worse, but still, whatever decision we're making is essentially locked in by the narrow perspective of our viewpoint. The only way we can "work" effectively is to change perspective.

The Vajrayana literature is founded in this holistic viewpoint, that everything that arises does so without cause and without aim; it simply arises as a function of the play of manifestation. There is a rhyme and a reason to that. It has a certain motion, and that motion is traceable. And, at the same time, to divide is to attempt to crystallize something that is inherently "un-crystallize-able," which of course is going to create conflict and suffering.

In our practice, "assertion" or the practice of "Just This," is like the ultimate Vajrayana practice, equivalent with *dzogchen*.[41] It defines whatever arises as completely essential only to its own arising. "Just This" disconnects everything from everything else.

This practice is something that we can bang our heads against, right from the beginning. There is no linearity; there is no time; there is no space. Whatever is, *is*, here and now, exactly and only.

So, what to do about that disconnection? Does that mean that our love for our children and our love of our creative life, or our professional lives, or our love of good food just sort of crumbles?

I read a book about Swami Vishuddhanand – a great yogi who was completely established in the nondual.[42] At a certain point, his guru told him to get married, to be in the world and serve the world; the implicit understanding being, "be in the world without losing your practice; without in any way falling under the illusion of the world."

---

41 According to some schools of Tibetan Buddhism, *dzogchen* (also known as the "Great Perfection") is the highest and most definitive path to enlightenment. It is the natural, primordial state or natural condition of every sentient being.
42 Gupta, Nand Lal, *Yogirajadhiraj Swami Vishuddhanand Paramahansadeva, Life & Philosophy*. Varanasi: Vishwavidyalaya Prakashan, 2004.

The phrase is "Just This." ... Just means nothing else – no options, no alternatives: Just This. What does that mean? It means that in reality, in fact, there isn't anything except Just This ... What Just This actually defines – what it is – is very powerful medicine to combat the sickness of separation, duality, illusion. It means Just – which means nothing else, exclusively, only – This; in the moment of repeating that phrase, it's whatever "This" is

... Not just that piss-ant little traffic jam that's keeping you from getting to the beach and it's your weekend of vacation, but the suffering of the whole world, the universe – gross, subtle, etheric, auric, astral, all of it. In the moment of saying or thinking Just This, that "This" stands for everything that is in this moment, everything that exists, including nonexistence, because in the domain of existence, there has to be the opposite, which is nonexistence ... .

When you say Just This, verbally, subtly, instinctually, you are Asserting the reality or the truth of Life, which included birth, death, maintenance, the whole thing ... .

... Just This means no past, no future, nothing else. Just This. Ouch, that hurts! One of the struggles of the path is that we keep trying to relate to reality based on the habit of relating to past and future. There is no such thing as the past, and there is no such thing as the future, except in our minds. The past did exist, but it doesn't now, and the future does not exist, therefore it's academic.[1]

---

1 *Hohm Sahaj Mandir Study Manual*, Vol. 3, Prescott, Arizona, Hohm Press, 2001, pp. 11, 15-16.

Vishuddhanand didn't want to be in the world. He wanted to stay at his guru's ashram and practice. Nonetheless, he did what his guru said. He found a wife and had three kids, and he set up a practice as some kind of healer. He interacted with the world. But also, he had a very rigorous practice. He ate a very simple diet. He locked himself in his room for a certain number of hours every night and practiced. He loved his children like anyone would love their children, one would assume, but at the same time he was completely established in this state of emptiness.

From the viewpoint of duality, we have a conflict, which is: "How can I be established in a state in which all things are equal and still have my preferences, my desires, my wishes, my hopes and my dreams?" And, from the perspective of duality, you can't answer that. From the viewpoint of duality I can't understand that eggplant is equal to asparagus. *I simply can't.* In no way is an eggplant equal to asparagus! Not to mention the equality of *dog shit*. Because, if you're in India and you're a yogi, that's the way you convince your disciples that all things are equal: you eat shit, maybe your own, or cow shit, or horse shit, or pig shit, or dog shit, or monkey shit if you live up in the mountains or in Rishikesh, where there are big monkeys. Then the disciples can't say, "That wasn't *really* shit; somebody left him a piece of bread."

One practices assertion, "Just This," as a way of increasing the irritation of the knowledge that no amount of practice can accomplish [this recognition of nonduality, of the emptiness and the equality of all things]. That friction or irritation is what creates intention and the spontaneous arising of assertion *as it is.*

Social Action or Not?

"What is the place of social action?" is one of the confu-
sions that tend to arise if we're really "thinking" about such
things (which I have come to the conclusion is totally a
waste of time) as separation and non-separation. That
is a very real question. A part of most of us feels deeply
empathetic with the suffering of others. If an opportunity
comes up to do something, to alleviate the suffering, of
course, most of us want to participate – whether that be
voting for somebody whom we feel has potential to really
bring some degree of consciousness to their tenure in office,
or whether it means marching for causes that have some
consciousness to them and are designed to help alleviate
the unjust suffering of others. In reality, however, there
is no conflict [in serving others while maintaining the
dharma of nonduality].

There is also no conflict when we are caught in a
serious health crisis. Suppose we go to the homeopath,
and then to the naturopath, and things don't seem to be
working. Do we tough it through, and throw ourselves
at the mercy of Yogi Ramsuratkumar? Well, what if
we've already done that, and things seem to be getting
worse? Then, do we go the allopathic route and suffer
the shame and the blame that any allopath will shower
on you for having wasted all the time you've "wasted"
drinking algae, eating seaweed and not having come
right away, the minute you discovered something, and
having organs cut out and your body forms severed?
(These surgeons are serious! And they're absolutely
convinced that even if you have the worst kind of viru-
lent cancer in the world, if only you'd come to them in

time, they could have saved you. Talk about an illusion! They could have saved you with enough chemo and radiation, of course.)

People are always asking me, what would *you* do in such a health crisis? Or, they ask, should I get surgery or not? But, there is a way of having an understanding of what I would do without asking me. In any conflict or any crisis, typically, when we are able to *view reality holistically*, meaning, when we are able to view reality without dividing it up, like: "nonduality ... and duality, and ... my practice, and ... days when I don't practice, and it's really *good* when I do this, but it's really *bad* when I do that ..." etcetera. When and if we are able to see reality continuously – as a continuous field of arising phenomenon – then the conflicts that we have within a divided world are seen in an entirely different light. The solution to those conflicts, not one-hundred percent of the time, but often, are crystal clear.

So, we don't have to go to the guru, or the scriptures, or to our meditation pillow, or to Yogi Ramsuratkumar in prayer, for the answers. Because, when we can see things holistically, then the perspective with which we are viewing whatever we are in conflict over is completely different. And, when the perspective is different, then obviously, what solutions might be brought to that conflict are completely different. Very much the way that you may look down at an image on a sheet of paper and see it with some depth perspective, but if the paper is turned sideways, you see that the image is contained on just a single sheet of paper. The radical difference with which you see that piece of paper is equal to the radically different way you would see the crisis that you are in.

Viewing Holistically

Were you able to see a crisis in a holistic field in which you were able to manage your mind, your mind would see the crisis from a completely different perspective; not necessarily a higher perspective, just a different perspective. And the perspective is so different that, what may have seemed completely confusing from one perspective now may have multiple solutions or options, when viewed from a different perspective.

One of my students was recently going through a health crisis. She saw all these expert doctors and nobody can figure out what it was. A friend of hers, another "expert" doctor, even e-mailed his "expert" doctor-friends describing this student's condition and asking them for their input. Now, every expert doctor is giving her a different solution to the situation. What to do?

Well, from a dualistic perspective, when your body is in as bad shape as her body was in, the obvious solution is: go to an expert; see an internist who can check your blood for things that nobody else would consider checking it for, or whatever. That's pretty much what all of us would think of. But, if you see the whole circumstance of the breakdown of your body from a radically different perspective – again, not necessarily higher, but different – a solution may present itself that has nothing to do with doctors and healing.

This student kept asking me what I thought was wrong with her, but I didn't know. Still, I do have a different perspective than that of simply going to doctor after doctor until somebody is able to help. (And my perspective is not to deny all medical help either. It's not to ignore the condition until you drop dead in your tracks.) And yet, there are different ways to approach any kind of healing process, or financial struggle, or moral issue. The optimal approach, the true approach, is to see whatever arises without division.

As long as we're proceeding dualistically, the response to any crisis is going to be defined by our worldview. Some people have a very broad worldview, while some people have a narrow worldview. When any kind of situation arises in our lives that is a conflict for us, we cannot meet the conflict as long as we see it from the viewpoint of division, or any other way that we've been trained to meet it. [For instance, if your son or daughter brings home a person of a different race, and introduces them as their boyfriend of girlfriend], we can say to ourselves, "I'm an adult, and my child is an adult and I've raised them to make their own choices and not to be prejudiced." We can take a couple of deep breaths and shake the person's hand, and say "Welcome to my home," even though we're going crazy. But, those actual internal responses to the circumstance can only be defined by our divided worldview.

In some psychological growth processes they talk about "seeing out of the box."[43] But, actually, we *can't* "see out of the box." The only way you can "see out of the box" is to *be* out of the box. As long as we're seeing things in the dividing way that we have been trained to see things, we can't see things from outside of the box.

Obviously, the question is how do you get outside of the box? If you're Timothy Leary, you take acid. If you're some yogi, you meditate for twenty years in a cave until every last remnant of lust and desire has been burned into a crisp, or suppressed. Both work equally well. If you can suppress

---

43 The "box" is another term for limited mind, programmed mind, or the small, tight confines of the status quo view of reality.

something well enough without suffering psychosomatic effects, more power to you.

I'm all for suppression! And, if you're able to maintain the suppression until you die, it's as good as having burned it to a crisp. Really ... it is! Most people can't, of course, because one-hundred years of suppression gives them a heart attack or a stroke. But, in academic terms, could you? Why not? The eclectic Bauls say, "If it works, use it." So, if it serves your sadhana, why not incorporate even suppression into your sadhana? If it helps your child to love you more by suppressing your tendency to dominate their lives and treat them like they're still three years old when they're teenagers, then suppression it is. I am all for suppression under those circumstances. I'd rather my children think I was a great guy, even if I thought they were making all the wrong choices in the world, by keeping my mouth shut, than if I was just another asshole, like every other person my age. What else, besides suppression, can you do when a situation arises with your children? Change your worldview? Yes, of course, but it's not that easy. By the time you change your worldview your kids are grown up and gone through college.

Fears of Nonduality

In the book *Dakini's Warm Breath*, Judith Simmer-Brown wrote:

> The highest realization is one in which gender dualities are seen as "not one, not two" and all apparent phenomena are understood for what they are. There is finally no projector, no projection, and no process of projecting. This is called *Mahamudra*, the great

symbol, in which all phenomena are merely symbols of themselves.[44]

She is not saying that phenomena don't exist. But, phenomena are what they are exactly, no more, no less. They don't point to anything, or indicate anything, or stand for anything. They just are what they are, and are symbols of themselves. That is the realization that we come to when assertion [the practice of Just This in Lee's teaching] is true of us: whatever arises is just what it is. Obviously we can still talk about things, because we have language and we like to talk; we are conversational beings and relational beings. But, when assertion – Just This – is true of us, we are not under the illusion that the implications and the directionality or spatiality that we give to things is, in fact, true of those things. Any thing is nothing but itself; exclusively only itself. All things are "symbols of themselves."

Different responses to different things will arise spontaneously in a state of nondual awareness. The relationship to violence will be different than our relationship to the creation of art, not because it's a moral issue, but because that's part of the vast intelligence of reality (but not "reality" as a being, or a thing). The vast intelligence of reality creates different relationships with different things based on what is in relationship to that thing. For instance, if you are a pornographic film producer, you will have a different relationship to certain forms of sex than if you are a parent with a daughter who is fourteen but who looks twenty-two. (You would have a different relationship to those things even if you and the pornographic film producer were both enlightened. So, it's not a moral question.)

---

44 Simmer-Brown, Judith, *Dakini's Warm Breath: The Feminine Principle in Tibetan Buddhism*. Boston: Shambhala, 2002, p. 16.

From a divided viewpoint, however, one of the things that scares us is that we don't want to see things equally. The mind says, "Aggression and violence are not equal to love and compassion." But, aggression and violence and love and compassion are all empty phenomenon, *and* with the realization of all things being equal we will not respond to aggression and violence as we will to love and compassion. We simply won't.

If we were yogis living in Tibet or India and the work was giving us the job to demonstrate a certain possibility of viewing all things equally, we might literally eat shit or glass, or we might do violence to somebody. When we read the books about these saints and hear some of these things, we may say, "Oh my God, this person is demonstrating this, that, or the other thing. I could never do that. I wouldn't want to do that. If this is going to be the result of my practice … I don't want it."

I remember once, years ago, going to an introduction to the *est* course.[45] A very attractive woman was making the presentation, and was so inspired by her own presentation in promoting the course that she got carried away. She was talking about realizing "things being equal," and she said that "… to me, sex and pancakes are exactly the same." Immediately, when she said that, she realized that she had just lost the crowd. "Well, not exactly the same, you have to understand this perspective," she tried to explain. But when people first heard her, their reactions were, "I'm not taking this course. I don't want sex to be the same as pancakes. No way! Except for the syrup!"

---

45 The *est* course, later known as The Forum, was developed by Werner Erhard. It is a powerful workshop experience in which individuals confront their basic assumptions about the nature of life and reality.

One of the things that actually handicaps our practice is this internal viewpoint that if I practice and realize that equality of all things, the texture of my life will completely disappear. I won't know the difference between my partner and my best friend's partner. I won't know the difference between my children and every child at the school they go to. We're afraid of that. So, we compromise our practice. But really, it's only philosophy that is disturbing us. We don't *know* that viewpoint of equality; we've read it in a book. And, from the viewpoint of duality, we have just as much possibility of compromising our practice because of *that* illusion as we do of practicing more ardently because we think we are going to be enlightened in three weeks.

Both illusions, both projections, compromise the clarity and integrity of our practice. It's not just negative illusions that compromise our practice, it is positive illusions too. All illusions compromise our practice. So, both things work against us. Part of us wants to practice and realize, the other part of us does not want to, because we have this fear, based in our dualistic worldview, our divisive worldview, that if we practice we are going to be this yogi-bump-on-a-log lost in some dream world in which we can't even pick our noses and chew our nails. And what fun would life be then? Or, we're afraid that we couldn't gossip anymore. Wouldn't that be a hell realm? If all things were equal, who could we find fault with? "Oh God, please don't give me that realization. You mean, I, Lee Lozowick, arrogant and superior, but objectively superior, as I am, would have to view myself equal to every slob on the street? No way. I am *not* going to practice!" Of course, those associations tend to be unconscious, but those are the things that really bind our practice.

Start Here

How can we practice rightly, meaning without dividing? What do we do in the beginning? Well, every time you find yourself dividing, manage your mind and don't divide. Just control your mind.

And if you say to yourself, "Yes, I can do that as an act of will, but that's not practice." I say, *we all have to start somewhere.* Start where you are. If you go into a yoga class and you look at an advanced instructor's postures, you may well say, "I'm never going to be able to do that, so the hell with it," and you may never start. Then, where are you going to be? Unhealthy and inflexible. What would any of us do if on the first day in French or Spanish class the teacher said, "These are the last words of English you are going to hear, because this class is going to be completely done in the language we want to learn." Certainly on that first day you are completely lost; you don't understand a thing. But, where would you be if you didn't stay in the class?

We have to start somewhere. When we find our mind dividing, we simply exercise an effort of will and we change the mind. Because it's the mind that divides, it's not the being. Our cells don't create division in perception. Instead of saying, "Oh, this isn't practice, this is fake," you change the mind. And when you change the mind enough, then the mind starts to get in line. Because the mind wants to be obedient. It's only doing the job it thinks it's supposed to do anyway. The mind thinks it's supposed to divide.

Get Out of the Way

The only thing that is going to make a difference is when we act on a kind of holistic, tacit knowledge. As long as we have to "think" something out, we will be more or less accurate, but our decisions will never be more than an educated guess. So, *we* are not going to make it work. It is going to work if we get out of our own way.

A lot of the instruction that comes down the pike is not about doing something active; it is about getting out of our own way. And sometimes the only way to get out of our own way is to be caught in a contradiction that stops the mind. Because, if the mind catches the contradiction, we're still in our own way. That was the whole principle of Gurdjieff's use of shock – it stopped the machine for a minute. And when the machine stops for an instant, the radiant shower of grace, which is always railing against the fortresses that we have built to keep it out – grace, mercy, wonder and majesty – gets in. As soon as the machine stops for an instant, *shweehuh*, all that stuff gets in. And if the machine stops for enough instances, and all of that stuff builds a certain charge, and we are willing to be resonant and responsive to that charge, then something can happen. Otherwise, nothing happens. Because we have got a lockdown on our personal and psychological interaction with the world. A lockdown!

E.J. Gold said years ago that our "character"[46] is perfect. It couldn't get any better. We aren't going to win against a perfect "character." The only way to win is to drop the present character entirely, and enter into a Work character that we create and we define and we build slowly, with the help of the dharma, the sangha, the teacher. That is the only way out.

---

46 *character*, as the term is used by E.J. Gold, refers to the role one takes up or position one assumes when engaging in a video game. One takes on a certain "character" with all its attributes, strengths and weaknesses, weapons of defense and so on, and then proceeds to play the game as that character. When the game is finished, one can take on another character.

There is no way out as long as we stay *in* the "character" that is a perfect *character*, that we have built personally and psychologically. That character has got a lockdown on our lives – every element of our lives, even when we're sleeping. Which is why dreams are useful, on occasion, because they give us hints to the character that we need to drop; hints that we don't get when we're awake, because it is a different energetic, different dynamic.

This is the basic point – there is *no way out* as long as we stay *in* the "character" – and the mind can't wrap itself around this. We have to hear it over and over and be "assaulted" by it, and eventually it gains a foothold, like James Bond hanging by his fingertips. And then, the next time we hear it we're holding on by our elbows. And then, we swing up, even though we've had our knees broken and our head smashed in … four concussions, eight broken ribs, guts practically hanging out. Still, like Bond, we can chase that bad guy down and beat him up!

CHAPTER 8

Managing Attention

The mind's judgment goes so fast. Yet, energy follows attention. If you put your attention on unity instead of division, and you just keep bringing your attention back there every time that you find that you've missed it ... *okay, you've missed, but just bring the attention back* ... then, slowly, you'll start building force toward *that*, toward unity, rather than toward the habit of judgment or division.

The mind doesn't work fast enough to catch that reflex of judgment, but the body does. So, if you keep putting your attention on the aim, so to speak, that's where the energy goes. And, then, over some time, the body will start slowing down the reflex so that you *can* catch it. You have to be patient and give yourself some time.

Suppose you have negative thoughts about other people, you address such things through the re-placing of attention. Don't take these thoughts seriously, as if they meant something about *you*; that they mean you are a bad person, or that you are not practicing. These thoughts don't mean anything about you. You picked those thoughts up from the conclusions you drew from an environment that was essentially hostile when you were a child. They're not *your* thoughts. They are not intrinsic to you. You didn't come up with any of that on your own. Those kinds of thoughts are reactive.

Such thinking is all a reactive process that has been conditioned into us from assumptions we made when we were little. You should take them seriously because you want to practice and earn merit, but you should not take them seriously as if those things you are observing are defining you, as if they are *who you are*. What defines you and who you are is "basic goodness."[47] And then there is all the "stuff" we have to work with.

We are continuous. We are always the same person. Don't take the states seriously because they are constantly shifting and moving.

The mind wants to monopolize every reaction (caused by any disagreement or a tone in someone's voice) and turn a molehill into a mountain. Every time we have a reaction, any kind of a reaction, what our mind wants to do is take the reaction, monopolize the emotions and the feelings and make a problem out of it.

We all have different degrees of ability to manage that problem-making process. If it is a small reaction, that doesn't strike at the core of our neurosis, and the mind does its thing, then it is easy to manage the mind relative to its desire to monopolize that reaction. It doesn't mean that much to us. But, if it is something that really strikes to the core of our "chief feature" [see footnote 17] then the intensity of the mind is that much stronger, and the intensity of our intention to manage the mind has to be that much stronger. Always, the first thing to do, literally, is to put our attention on something else.

---

47 "basic goodness," the term used by Chögyam Trungpa Rinpoche to describe the Buddha-nature of all beings.

With my second daughter I spent a lot of time raising her. I was often taking care of her when her mom went out. Occasionally, maybe even more than occasionally, I had this idea in my mind that I would be with her for a couple of hours. But if her mom lost all sense of time, sometimes it would be three, four, or five hours before she would come home. Then, I would get annoyed and start thinking negatively about her. The way I stopped that was to put my attention on the child. And always, it worked like a charm. Every time! Whenever I would put my attention on my daughter, my own building negativity dissolved. Any time we put our attention on something that pleases us, something that we like, something that serves us or someone else, something that we really enjoy, that just fills the field of our consciousness.

In any situation of reactivity, the first thing you can do is put your attention on one of the children (children work fabulously) or on something that happened during the day that you really like: a client who came in and said something wonderful to you. You can literally force your attention onto that, and start a whole different mood in the body. You may have to do that several times, because what the mind really wants to do is put its attention on the reaction that you've had and use that reaction to maintain its authority. That's what ego wants to do. So you may have to replace your attention a couple of times. But, pretty soon that's where your attention will be − on whatever it is that's creating feelings of pleasure and gratitude and anticipation and enjoyment, and then you're earning merit instead of un-virtue.

Place Attention on the Guru

Dudjom Rinpoche[48] said, "It is easier to act in ways that earn merit than to act in ways that are unvirtuous." If you really think about that statement it's shocking. We often think that to do things that earn merit we have to go against our personal wishes, and the dictates of ego, and our psychological labyrinth. We have this idea: "I'm self-centered, and I think of myself first, and I want comfort. I don't want to be that way, but that's the way I am. I'm completely mechanical, I've been practicing for fifteen years and nothing has changed." Thinking of ourselves in those terms we think of doing acts that produce merit as being something that we have to make an effort to do.

Rinpoche also said that one of the best ways to earn merit was to simply turn our attention to the guru, or to remember our devotion to the guru. Anytime we polarize with someone – it can be about anything, like the fact that somebody else is higher up on the hierarchical ladder than we are, and it is very disturbing, especially when we think that we have something to say that has merit and should be considered equally – the first thing to do is to literally put our mind on something else.

> *Deepening surrender to the Master is not found in obeying the mind.* – Lee Lozowick, September 1999

---

48 His Holiness Dudjom Rinpoche, Jigdrel Yeshe Dorje (1904-1988), was the supreme head of the Nyingmapa Order. Poet, author of many books, *terton* (visionary discoverer of hidden teachings), historian, meditation master and tantric yogi, he was one of the most beloved and grandfatherly of the grand lamas of Tibet.

Label It

Questioner: When my mind is obsessing on something, and I've actually got a physical thing going on, my mind is beyond thinking. I'm actually in a physical, chemical state where I literally feel that I'm going to explode.

Lee: That's true. A strong enough reaction will create chemical reciprocity in the body.

Questioner: But it feels like once I get to that spot, my physical body is so far gone, so involved, that I can't simply alter my attention.

Lee: It is not "so far gone." It just *feels* that way, instinctually.

If you find yourself in that state and you're able to label the state: "This is a chemical state. This is chemistry ... body chemistry. This is a glandular reaction," you *will* be able to stop it, or at least take steps to minimize it. But you have to label it: "This is just chemistry." If you say, "Oh my God I'm overwhelmed," then obviously you are overwhelmed.

If you can have enough presence of mind to say, "This is chemistry, the body has been taken over by chemistry," then you can put your attention on something that initiates a counter-chemical secretion in the body. Any glandular secretion has to process through the system, but there are anti-toxins within the body. When the body creates chemistry that puts it into that kind of hyperstate, these are anti-toxins that will quiet it down. You just have to trigger that.

Questioner: So, you are saying that it is better to focus on something else rather than trying to change the dynamics of the situation?

Lee: Realistically speaking, what are the odds of changing it?

Questioner: *Very little.*

Lee: Exactly! Clearly, if you are in a situation with somebody, or a non-human situation, in which there is a fair probability that if you spoke up, took a stand, grabbed the person and said "Hey, come on!" that something might change, then maybe you take a risk and you go for it. Or, like Milarepa and the final demon of his meditation retreat, if you can enter into and embrace what it is that you've polarized toward, fine. But, if you can't embrace it in this way, then you can still turn a negative situation into something that can earn merit by placing your attention elsewhere.

Most of us are just too plugged in to welcome the situation with equanimity. And that's the key – to welcome the situation! But if we bite our lip as we "welcome the situation" and we are still furious, it is not the same. We have to be able to welcome the situation with equanimity. Most of us really aren't able to do that, at our level of practice (and I certainly include myself in that). In most situations, the probability of change is very small. But, depending upon the situation, every once in a while you take a chance.

Wiggle Your Toes

Being able to "eat it" – that is, to work internally with a strong emotional situation – may take many years of practice. Overall, it is better to keep things to yourself and work them out *inside* than to just speak out of hand. As long as the process is correct – this process of cathexis – you keep doing it until it is effective. But, [while you are attempting to work things out inside], do something that is completely relaxing for five minutes. Go outside and throw yourself in the grass. Consciously tense the muscles and then relax them. Shake your hands and shake the stuff out. The simplest approach – which is really a band-aid approach, but it will always work if you need temporary relief [from some situation of high emotional reactivity, such as fear], which might mean days or weeks – is to wiggle your toes! Wiggling your toes won't in any way make the fear go away, it won't get to source, but it will handle the symptoms, and sometimes … why not? And then, don't stop wiggling your toes until you feel better.

Or you can count mantra on your fingers. Make sure that you are counting on your fingers – you have to actually put your mind there. Count your fingers and maintain the count, and every time you lose count, which you will, then just go back and start over. Those actions will take care of the extreme reactivity, just like that.

But again, that is not an ultimate solution. It won't really address the fear, but it will handle the symptoms. Sometimes, once the symptoms are handled, the emotional state doesn't come back for awhile. But, in terms of getting to the core of the thing … more practice! More meditation! And patience.

Sometimes when you break the actual feeling of fear, which you do by wiggling your toes, then also the feeling of being willing to take a risk will not be repressed. The consequences of a band-aid approach might be very significant. It might be actually the very thing you need to start getting closer to the core of it.

Somebody told me that little trick about the toes. They said that in the Air Force, the first thing they teach jet pilots is that whenever anything distracts you from handling the plane, including motion sickness, fear, anything … wiggle your toes. The guy who told me that was a jet pilot in the Air Force, and he said it always worked. The whole plane might be shaking, and he would be, not just afraid but, ready to throw up all over the instrument panel, and if he just wiggled his toes, it worked every time, like a charm. So, if it's good enough for the Air Force …!

It will work every time. But, you have to keep your attention on keeping your toes going, until you are feeling more relaxed and clear. Usually, by that time, your attention has moved so far that the fear doesn't come right back. Occasionally it will come back, but not usually.

Focus Attention on the Source

A student admitted to Lee that, when she doesn't get what she wants, sometimes her response is violence.

Lee: How clearly do you see the part of yourself that is committed to getting what it wants? Observing the violent reaction is fine, of course, but it is not like observing the source of the reaction. So, the more closely you can get to observing the actual source of the arising of something, the more probability there is that things will change. Not that *you* will change things, but that things will change.

Again, energy follows attention, so that's where you want to put your attention – at the source. And, of course, the source of the arising is much more subtle than the reaction. Reactions are much more gross. Instead of putting your attention on the reaction, put your attention on the source of the reaction, the cause of the reaction.

This takes some practice. It's not like the first time you do it … *okay, finished, success* … because it is very subtle. On the other hand, there is this thing that we call "beginner's luck." And sometimes the first time you try something, because you're kind of innocent relative to it, it works like a charm. And then, you have to sort of run to keep up, because immediately the mind clicks in and says, "Okay, now I've won. How can I keep winning?" And then the whole thing falls apart.

By the time there is a reaction, you're only looking at the consequence. Work with putting your attention on the source of the situation, rather than the result of the situation. Define the situation for yourself, but instead of letting your attention drift to the reaction, never mind the reaction when it's not there. (So, now you're not in a reaction, we're just talking about it.) Keep your attention on, "Where is this whole mechanism coming from?" ... keep it on the mechanism of wanting something, getting frustrated because you don't get it, and then there is a reaction.

CHAPTER 9

Mind in the Now

Repairing the Past

Even at the most superficial level of mind, it's probably obvious that to punish yourself for the rest of your life for a mistake in the past would be unnecessary. So, the idea of acceptance relative to things in the past is that, "They're the past. We can't do anything about them. All we can do something about is *now*."

It's sort of like the process of karma. The decision you make *now* reverberates, but it doesn't go backwards. Whatever has happened has happened. And it has no authority or power, except the authority or power we give it.

No matter how critical our experiences and our acts have been in the past, they're over. If we are different now, then life responds. People around us don't necessarily respond, however. In America there's a whole program for ex-inmates of prison to get jobs in the ordinary world, and it's very difficult because people don't trust them. Particularly if their crime was a violent one, people are scared of them, and scared that they are still violent.

There is no accounting for other peoples' opinions. Other people may never forgive you, or forgive any of us, for our past. There is nothing we can do about that. We can't change other peoples' minds. We can only change our own minds.

If there is any part of the work that you're doing that revolves around other peoples' opinions, the first thing to do is get rid of that [obsession with the opinions of others], because you can only deal with yourself. The past is finished! There is nothing we can do about it. We can't make up for it. But, you can live from the present. If in the past any of us have been selfish and lacking in generosity, we can't make up for that. But we can start being generous now, including being generous to ourselves.

Work with the idea that the past is finished ... *over*! I'm always having students come to me and apologize for the past. And it doesn't mean anything to me. Once something is over – sometimes I have a momentary negative reaction if somebody really messes up some project I gave them, or something – once it's finished, it's done. I'm on about the next project.

So, when people ask, "I'm really sorry I did that ... will you ever trust me again?" What a waste of time and energy! Every day is a new day, and never mind what happened a week ago, or ten years ago. Cultivate that relationship to the past – that is, it's finished, done.

If you're going to have a bunch of friends, what kind of friends do you want? Friends who are going to hold your past against you and never forgive you, or friends for whom the past is past; for whom the past doesn't mean anything? Obviously, the kind of people that you would like to be in relationship with (like Arnaud Desjardins), and like to be friends with, won't care about your past.

The "Child" in the Past

At a seminar in France in July 2007 another woman admitted to feeling violent reactions when she didn't get what she wanted.

Questioner: *I see my reactions, but am not able to see the source of the reactions. I am able to see the projections I make on my partner. I know where that comes from. It comes from my past. From lacking a mother. Part of me is that little girl who didn't get what she wanted. Didn't get to have a mother. And she didn't get the affection and love she wanted at that moment. That little girl is present. I can feel her.*

Lee: Okay, so that is a very accurate, intellectual description. Nobody could argue with it. And it is also an excuse for not seeing more clearly and more deeply. Where is the little girl that you are talking about?

Questioner: *I don't know.*

Lee: Exactly. Because she doesn't exist any more.

Questioner: *Yes, but there is a part of me that is demanding, expecting, wanting. And that part has been with me for years.*

Lee: But that part doesn't have to be here, because the little girl is not here anymore. And it is the little girl that is completely irrational. The little girl didn't get it, and the little girl is not here any more. And you probably are getting it, and not able to feel satisfaction in getting it because you're still giving the little girl power and authority.

At this point the little girl is just a fantasy. She doesn't exist. She's an idea. So, send her where she belongs – to the "Museum of Old Ideas" that are no longer relevant.

That's not the kind of direction like, "Here's a hammer, here's a nail; now nail the nail …" It's not that kind of physical circumstance. But, at the same time, you *can do that* by looking for the little girl, and seeing if you can find her. And when you can't find her, then you have a different kind of sense of yourself, and then something different can happen. But that has to be an experiential process, not a kind of intellectual process, which is part of what the Lyings process was developed for, to get somebody out of their head and into their experience.

Mind in Denial

Another woman recently told me that she too couldn't be happy because her "inner child" was wounded, hurting. I said, "The child is no more, so stop treating the child as if they still are." It was all a memory, and she was keeping the memory alive, and turning the memory into a hologram. She was making the memory a real thing, when it was just a specter, a ghost; it had no substance. But, she was still giving it substance, filling it up. I told her that she needed to see the insubstantiality of those ghosts profoundly enough so that she didn't fall into the same trap that crazy people fall into.

If we don't know what stars we are chasing, which is another way of saying "What do we really want?" and we think that we aren't chasing stars, when in fact we are, then we've got a very big obstacle between us and the path, the teaching, the sangha and the guru. The question, "What do I really want?" is really a very important question because such questions are intended to provoke peoples' clarity relative to any level of denial that they are in. This woman could have been happy even without the circumstances of her life changing. We could all be happy with things as they are, even though we are in pain with things as they are.

My instruction to "be happy" is an instruction to clarify a situation. I don't mean the formal content of a situation, but to clarify a situation so that we come to an understanding that the pain may be, in many cases, unnecessary. If the pain is unnecessary, and we were able to drop the pain, there would be happiness, in some form, mild, or otherwise ... or manic.

People often say that with me they "never know what is going on." But, despite what they say, one of the problems is that they really think that they *always* know. This puts them at odds with other people, who do know better, and other people who know less but who think they know more, and it also puts them at odds with their heartfelt desire to serve, because *thinking they know* precipitates actions that aren't coming from the guru or teacher, but are coming from our interpretation of the guru.

As long as we are using the mind to decide what to do, we aren't going to handle things. This complex of "I" that is stubborn and rigid and everything else, is not going to handle things. Because, whatever our habits are, they going to be with us until the day we die, no matter how hard we work and no matter even if we put in another seventeen years of psychotherapy.

Living in the Present Moment

Questioner: *I have difficulty in living in the present moment; I am constantly going into daydreams.*
Lee: What if "living in the present moment" meant daydreaming in that moment?

What I'm implying is that we often reject the present moment because what is arising in the present moment doesn't seem very "present" to us. Most of us aren't "present" all the time in the context with which we could define "Presence." What about all the time when we are not in that "Presence" state? Does it mean we are not present? No, of course not. The practice is to be with *what is, as it is, here and now.* That phrase does not say, "Accept what is, as it is, only when you feel that it is 'Presence' within the most enlightened definition of the word 'Presence.'" The practice is to *accept what is*. It doesn't say, "Accept *what is*, except the exceptions." There are no exceptions! *Accept what is* – which includes anything, when that's *what is* in the moment – *as it is*. Meaning, if it is purely relative in the moment, then that's what *it is, as it is* – relative! If it's imagination, projection, daydreaming, that's *what it is*. Accept what is, as it is, here and now. Whenever we come up with a concept that defines "enlightenment," "reality," "truth," ... and we aim for *that* definition in every moment, of course we are not going to find it.

If you have a mind – which we all have, even though sometimes we act like we don't, particularly when we're drunk or carried away by reactive emotions – there are times in the stream of consciousness when we are going to be daydreaming, projecting, living in the past. And, what removes any element of relativity from the domain of the false is the acceptance of that element of relativity *as it is*, relative!

Try it. When you catch yourself daydreaming, or whatever it is, instead of saying to yourself, "I'm not present, I want to be present," simply be present *as you are*, which in that case is daydreaming.

A Lively Dialogue About Now

Questioner: *I have the impression I'm sorting out many things in my life.*
Lee: Are you, or are you not?
Questioner: *Yes, it is real. In fact, it's real.*

Lee [with a provocative tone]: I heard you the first time.

Questioner: ...

Lee: Just kidding. Boy, the first time I tried that with you [in a previous seminar], you almost cut my head off. So, thank you for being different.

Questioner [with composure]. My impression is that I'm going nowhere.

Lee: If you *were* going somewhere, where would you be going?

Questioner: Paradise.

Lee: [Laughing] ... Oh well. If you figure out the route there, please let me know. Would you know if you got there?

Questioner: Well precisely.

Lee: Precisely ... what?

Questioner: Concretely speaking I have the impression I'm going nowhere, that I'm missing something?

Lee: Why? You haven't answered my question. "Would you know Paradise if you'd found it?"

Questioner: I'd like to know.

Lee: Yeah, but if you don't *know* what it is, how do you know you don't have it now? Ever read those science fiction stories where the person goes to heaven but it's completely opposite to what they thought heaven was, so they think it's hell? So they go to the boss and they say, "I don't like it here. I want to get out of this place. How do I get out of here?"

And the boss says, "What do you mean you don't like this place, what's the problem with it?"

And the person says, "I want to go to heaven. I'm a good person. I've led a good life. I want to go to heaven."

And the boss says, "You *are* in heaven."

Questioner: So then there is no problem. [She laughs.]

Lee: [Noting the woman's reaction, Lee comments] Boy, you're really loose, are you drunk? You've really changed. I'm not kidding!

Questioner: [*Now laughing uncontrollably.*]

Lee: See, now you're in Paradise. Anybody who is laughing like that … You're in Paradise!

Questioner: [*more laughter, all around*]

Lee: That was fast. You've made it. Ah, my most successful case to date.

[*More laughter.*]

Questioner [*regaining her breath*]: It's afterward that I'm going to feel like catastrophe has happened.

Lee: [Laughing.] That's even funnier. Why? You're having a good time. What are you some kind of a nun from the Middle Ages? You're going to go to whip yourself after? "Oh dear, I laughed too much today. I'm think I need to suffer."

There's no problem, why make a problem? At least there is no problem *now*. If you insist on creating a problem I'm afraid there is nothing I can do about it. But you don't have to! Try it. Try not vivifying a problem. It might seem a little strange at first, since if we have a habit of creating problems, as soon as we stop creating them we feel ill at ease; like something is wrong. But, it is obvious that if we have two options – problem and no problem – the better of two options is no problem. If we stay with this option, after a while it feels comfortable and it fits. It's a viable option, why not? What do you think? I mean the real question is, "What do you *feel?*" But, "What do you think?" is probably more fun of an answer. So?

Questioner: *I feel it is appropriate.*

Lee: Great! Thank you.

Ordinary Magic

Don't cultivate the need for certainty. Cultivate receptivity, maybe with a touch of wonder.

Often people say to me, "I've had this really scary experience," or "I've had this really scary dream," and actually the dream or experience is some kind of wonderful journey into some mystical realm. But, because it is so different from their ordinary reality, they take the gift of that experience as something scary instead of awesome or magical.

In Tibetan there's a word *drala,* which translates very loosely as "ordinary magic." What it means, also very loosely translated, is that in every moment of life there is the possibility for magic; and magic is translated as the immediacy of the presence of reality, here and now.

"Magic" doesn't mean some fantastic occurrence – lightning storms, and angels flying around your head whispering in your ear. The way tantric practitioners of Tibetan Buddhism use that word, magic is exactly *the acceptance of what is, as it is, here and now.* And they call that *drala.*

In that acceptance there is wonder and magic. Anything is possible! The expanse of life opens up in front of you, instead of closes down to a tiny aperture. (Which, by the way, is the first time I've ever used that word in English, "aperture." So I just want you all to appreciate that. The first time I've used that word in sixty-three years, so that makes all of you special.)

Chögyam Trungpa Rinpoche says that part of tantric practice is to cultivate drala as a state of being. When possible, it helps to cultivate a sense of the possibility of life, rather than the oppressiveness of life; to cultivate the possibility of wonder in every moment.

One of my students who rarely has any sort of vision-ary experience, was sitting in our meditation hall one day, twenty years ago. She looks down and there is an eight-centimeter image of Krishna dancing on her big toe. She rubs her eyes, and opens her eyes, and closes them again, and there is Krishna, still dancing on her big toe, playing his flute and looking all blue and sexy.

She was thrown into a state of wonderment, and when she described it afterward, she said, "It was really *real*. It was *really* real." And fortunately she didn't take that experience out of context and go into business as a Divine Mother, because many people start teaching on the basis of less than that.

The Universe is an infinitely multi-faceted reality and who knows what wonders could move through our lives if we relaxed and cultivated a sense of possibility instead of oppressiveness. Not that everybody goes through life feeling oppressed ... but we have lots of various responses.

To cultivate a sense of the wonder of possibility is to start to touch this quality of *drala*, recognizing that magic is not something that you have to run after; not something that only happens now and then; like: "Okay, now! I'm going to accept what is as it is here and now. I know I can do it now! There is nobody around to bother me. It is quiet. I have money in the bank. I'm healthy. Okay, now I'm gonna do it." No, *drala* is possible in every moment. Any moment is a moment *to accept what is, as it is, here and now.* You don't have to wait for special times when you're really feeling enthusiastic about practice, or when you're really feeling sharp. Every moment is another moment of possibility. That's *drala*, everyday magic; or, we could say, every *moment* magic. Cultivate that.

How do you cultivate something? You think about it, you consider it, you contemplate it. You try to practice it. You wonder what it means. You keep it in front of you. That's how you consider it. Whatever that means to you. You keep it present. Okay?

Part II
EMOTIONS

CHAPTER 10

Working With Emotions

You Are Not Your Emotions

Observing ourselves – that is, seeing *what is* – is about sweeping away the veils that maintain the illusion of our lives. When we see clearly, then there are no illusions. There are only illusions when we see in a cloudy way. In the domain of emotions, people commonly speak of "having" an emotion. But the truth of the matter is that we don't "have" emotion, and we can't have emotion. The truth of the matter is that we *believe* we have emotion and that's a complete illusion. It's a lie. Emotion arises, and we cling to it as if it were ours. It is our misunderstanding, our misinterpretation, our misidentification that claims the emotion as ours and identifies with it as if it were us. But it isn't.

Emotion can arise and emotion can subside, and we can simply watch it without allowing it to affect the body and the body's manifestations. It's not a matter of sitting on it and forcing it down, it's simply a matter of observing it arise and subside.

Thoughts, emotions and feelings are like waves on the ocean. The waves crash on the shore, and then the waves recede. In its natural state, no thought and no feeling and no emotion lasts very long. It's only when we take it and identify with it that it goes on and on. When something bothers us – we have a thought, for instance – we then obsess and obsess and obsess. The reason that thought is simply not subsiding and passing away is because we are holding onto it; not because we *want* to hold onto it, but because we believe that thought to actually *be* who we are.

We say "I think," "I feel," "I emote," but really we don't, we only believe we do. We've identified ourselves with this mind-body complex so that anything that arises in the mind-body complex we assume, automatically and unconsciously, that it's us. *And it's not us.* It's simply that within the mind-body-complex thoughts, emotions and feelings arise and subside.

We are prior to or transcendent to all of it – all of it, even love. "*Oh no, not that!*" Yes, even love. We are prior to all of it. When we're able to make that distinction, not in our mind or in our emotions or in our feelings, but in the one thing that is constant and unchangeable, which is consciousness, then we can observe thoughts, emotions and feelings arise and subside without feeling the necessity to *do* something about them. That's one of the aims of spiritual practice.

Instead of using the mind to analyze what's arising, such as, "I'm feeling angry and I shouldn't. Anger is not a good emotion." Or, "I'm really enjoying taking this power and that's not so good," we should not waste our time. Instead, we can simply *observe* what is arising from the surface to the depth of things. Because, in that observation there is knowledge and wisdom. In mental analysis there is only opinion and subjectivity – sometimes our opinion is accurate, sometimes it is inaccurate; either way, it's just opinion.

Knowledge is in the depth of our being and we get to knowledge through observation – clear, honest, unbiased observation.

If we are observing clearly, what we will see (maybe not right away but if we continue to process) is that "I" is never angry. We will see that anger arises in a constellation that surrounds but does not interpenetrate "I."

"I" is pristine and untouched by anything. Although like a magnet drawing filings to it, it has accumulated this whole galaxy of qualities, of emotions, of thoughts, of expectations that arise and subside based on the physics of the situation. Then, distinctions can be made based on the reality of the situation rather than based on the illusion of the situation. Every time we find ourselves starting to think, "I'm getting angry," we can say, "Wait a minute, anger is arising." Then, the natural question that comes after that is, "From where? Where is anger arising?" So we will naturally be drawn toward an observation and realization of the way things are essentially.

Emotions vs. Feelings – a Distinction

Although we (and I include myself in this) commonly use the term "emotion" to apply to both feelings and emotions, there is a real difference between a feeling and an emotion. A feeling is simply what arises in response to something, and an emotion is what we "do" – what mood we animate based on the feeling. There are positive emotions and negative emotions. The positive ones are happiness, joy, delight, wonder, and so on. The negative ones obviously include anger, frustration, despondency, disillusionment.

It takes a lot of energy to animate emotions – positive *or* negative emotions, because even positive emotions can eat up energy. To be able to feel, and stay with the feeling, but not necessarily follow the impulse to do something

with it (to animate emotion) is a way to contain and con‑
serve energy.

Obviously there are different types of people: a *sattvic*
type and a *rajasic* type are not going to act the same.[49] The
sattvic type is going to be cool and self‑contained, and the
rajasic type is going to be fiery and gregarious. I'm not
talking about the difference in types, but about indulging
in emotional activity when you could simply stay with the
feeling. The feeling is what's essential anyway. Emotion
gets superimposed on feeling and sometimes actually quite
complicates it.

Often, when we say "I'm feeling happy," it's actually
that we are emotionally happy; and we *may* also be feel‑
ing happy. But often we are disconnected. We are so used
to experiencing emotions as feelings that often we think
that we are feeling, and we may be feeling something very
similar, but actually we're articulating an emotion and call‑
ing it feeling.

This is a very delicate issue because one can go too far
to the other side. One can detach oneself from relationship
altogether and then say to oneself, "Well, I'm not emoting,
I'm *observing*." If you go to many Fourth Way Groups, par‑
ticularly traditional Fourth Way Groups, you'll see people
sitting around watching everything, being completely unin‑
volved, and that's their idea of containing their emotions. In
effect, that may just be being out of relationship.[50]

---

49 The three *gunas* – or primary forces of creation – are the *sattvic*, the *rajasic* and the
tamasic. Sattvic (*sattva*) refers to the condition of illumination, clarity, serenity; *rajasic*
(*rajas*) to motion, energy and activity, and *tamasic* (*tamas*) to restraint and inertia.
50 Fourth Way Groups – based in the work of G.I Gurdjieff. He called his approach
the "Fourth Way" because it incorporated and went beyond the three previously
demonstrated paths: that of the monk, the fakir and the yogi. This practice places strong
emphasis on rigorous self-observation and the practice of the non-expression of negative
emotions.

Distinguishing between the things that eat up "work energy" and the things that contain and build work energy is important.[51] Reactions to things eat up work energy. The observation of things without *reacting* (which doesn't mean you don't *act*) tends to build and contain work energy. Hard physical labor, even though it may exhaust the body, doesn't necessarily exhaust work energy. But, if you are working hard physically and complaining the whole time, that's going to use up work energy.

I used to take a martial arts class, and when some exercise was hard I used to grunt, because it made it easier. At one point the teacher said, "No sound." To contain the tendency to grunt or make some noise made me exercise harder, but in the long run made the body more effective because it contained energy instead of expressing energy.

If you are at a football game, and your team makes some great play, intercepts a pass and runs it all the way to a touchdown, you jump up, screaming and yelling, and maybe throwing popcorn all over! Whatever you do vents a tremendous amount of raw energy – energy that could be used for work. It doesn't mean that we can't be happy, enthusiastic, pleased and tremendously excited by the fact that our team is doing well, but there is a way of enjoying without jumping up and down, screaming and waving our arms. Some of that will vary based on type. So, a *rajasic* type will be more expressive than a *sattvic* or *tamasic* type. It's a matter of being able to rest in that space between feeling and acting, and then the distinctions become clear.

---

51 work energy – A term borrowed from Fourth Way, referring to the accumulated energetic substance, stored in the body-mind complex, used to further intentional practice. Gurdjieff said: "All energy spent on conscious work is an investment; that spend mechanically is lost forever."

Response vs. Reaction

Arnaud Desjardins created distinctions with his sangha about the "active passive" and the "passive active." The "passive active" is when you act without motive. Your action is simply a function of response to the circumstance. A lot of people misunderstand Arnaud's teaching about "accept what is *as it is*." They think that "to accept" means no action. They think, "I am going to 'accept what is *as it is*' and stay here like a vegetable." But, Arnaud draws a distinction between responding and reacting. Ordinarily, we react; a kind of nervous thing. And when we react, of course, we aren't going to bring consciousness to the situation, so people think that they have to snuff or stuff the reaction. But they aren't making the distinction between "responding" and "reacting."

If you are on an airplane that runs off the runway and bursts into flames, and you are "accepting what is *as it is*," then to react would be to start screaming and calling for your mother. To respond would be to get up, see if you are hurt, see who needs help and go about helping the staff get people out off the airplane. But, often, we think that "to accept what is *as it is*" is to be completely passive. "Oh the plane is running off the runway and is bursting into flames ... Therefore my time has come and I am going to sit here and accept my death *as it is*," which is never what Arnaud means or what he talks about. His teaching is always: "Respond, don't react!" To react is an unconscious mechanism. To respond is a natural and spontaneous action that is based on inner resolve, not on unconsciousness, psychological habit, life script, childhood trauma, or whatever else creates the reaction, like fear, raw fear.

A response does not require investigation. Simply, we look around, we see what is wanted and needed, and we provide that. Werner Erhard said once that whenever he walked through Central Park in New York City and he saw garbage on the grass, he picked it up. Then, when he got to a trashcan, he put the garbage in the trash. He went on to say that of course there were people who got paid by the city to clean the garbage, but still this was a public park, full of beauty, and people are supposed to enjoy it, and it didn't hurt him to pick up the trash; it was not a problem to bend down and put something in his pocket or in a bag. He was there anyway.

That's the idea of a natural response. You don't have to have any great sophistication. You don't have to understand the ins and outs of the Public Sanitation Department of New York City. You simply need to pick up the trash and put it in a trashcan when you come to one.

Response is a very natural, obvious interaction with the circumstance as it needs to be. One of my students was walking along the street in India and saw a man beating his daughter. My student rushed in and stopped the man from beating his daughter, and this catalyzed a reaction by the man's entire clan. They were literally going to kill him (my student). Luckily, somebody came along who knew the family and knew my student, and was able to take the fuel out of the situation.

Certainly, nobody wants to see a child suffer. If most of us considered the situation, we would be brokenhearted, pierced with the suffering of the circumstance, and we would feel for that little girl. And if we stopped to think and consider the whole situation, we might go in and try to reason with the father to stop the beating of the child. However, even when we do the right thing (and what my student did *may* have been the right thing to do, I don't know), if the motive for that action is reactivity, blind reactivity, then there cannot help but be some conflict there.

Once, one of the children swallowed a big piece of hard candy and she was starting to turn blue. Luckily she was with her mother, who immediately held her upside-down and whacked her on the back, and the candy came out. So, if that's a reaction, God bless the reaction! This child's mother did the right thing! In the consideration of consciousness, however, even when we do the right thing we still have a further aim, which is to do the right thing as a response to the circumstance not as a reaction to the circumstance. And that's a very important distinction.

To never react is probably unrealistic and unnatural. But if we're self-observing with any degree of clarity, and we notice a reaction, and we've already reacted, we can't suck it back in. We can, however, sever the ongoing habit to indulge the reaction, or to keep blaming the person, or to stay angry. And we will consider these possibilities in greater depth throughout this book.

Even in a more serious situation – like if a doctor says you are going to have lose your leg – it's not that there wouldn't be a shock of recognition, or a natural grieving process. But I'm speaking of emotional reaction that's unnecessary. If we have a shock we *will* have an initial reaction, but then: "Okay, this is reality, what do I need to *do?*" "Who do I need to speak to?" "How do I need to establish myself given this new information?" It's not that all feeling goes dead. We have an initial reaction, but then we go into "let's-deal-with-this" mode.

With Every Emotion – Not to React!

If you pick out any particular emotion as if it were different from all the other emotions, then you're going to have a lot more difficulty dealing with it. So, yes, some emotions are more provocative, more vital than others, and still we approach practice relative to every emotion the same. Jealousy, for example, is like any other emotion.

For people for whom jealousy is a problem, who want to handle it so that it doesn't imbalance them, or so that they don't lose control and chop somebody's head off, verbally or physically, most of those people would never find happiness or sentimentality to be in the same category. But, if you take someone who is wildly, passionately jealous, and see them with a baby, or a puppy or a kitten, they may very well be going, "*Ohhhh*, you're *sooo* cute. *Ohhh, boo, boo, boo, boo.*" If you say to that person, "That reaction (of sentimentality) is the same thing as your reaction to jealousy," they will say, "What are you talking about? It's not the same thing." But it is! So, you approach every emotion the same way: you ask, "What is it?"

They used to have this exercise to get rid of headaches in Werner Erhard's course, and I'll share it with you in case any of you want to try it. You look at the headache and you say, "What shape is it? What color is it?" And then, as soon as you do that, you say it again. By the time you realize that headaches have no shape and no color, the headache is gone. You realize that something that you're making a "thing" isn't thing; it is nothing! It's a reaction.

So, every emotion is a reaction. *We* give them substance. *We* give them reality, body power, authority, when in fact they are nothing. They are reactions. If you start to look at any emotion by asking, "What is it? Where does it come from?" ultimately you will find that it is just a reaction. And, you will find that it is just as possible *not* to react as it is to react.

Obviously, given peoples' different psychological labyrinths, different people react to different things with different degrees of force. In fact, sometimes when we're taken over we'll actually say, "I was carried away, I couldn't help myself." People are afraid of being out of control, especially with emotions like rage and jealousy. Their argument is, "I can't just watch it, I might kill somebody. I might smash my partner over the head with a bottle or an iron pot." But the thing is, if you are *really* seeing it, you'll see what it is. And in seeing what it is, the reaction will not continue uncontextualized.

Before the point of being carried away it's just as easy not to react as it is to react. Once we're carried away, we're carried away. Still, some of you have probably had the experience: You're in the middle of a reaction, you're carried away, and yet something stops you. Maybe you're fighting with your partner furiously, and all of a sudden something in your peripheral attention captures your attention, and you turn around and you see the look on the face of your child. Instantly, you're able to stop the wave. Your response to your child is more important than staying with your reaction.

Well, you can have that kind of response before the reaction gets a grip. When you feel jealousy (or any other strong emotion) arising – and if you're paying attention you can feel it starting to crank up and build momentum – then the question is, "What is this?" We always know when such a thing is happening; it doesn't sneak up on us by surprise.

There is a concept that whatever you struggle against gains strength. If you fight against an emotion, you give it power. Every time you react to the reaction, you're empowering the reaction – that is, giving the first reaction authority or power over you. So, when you catch yourself in reaction, you don't want to react to the reaction. You want to *see* the reaction … the first reaction. And the way you see it is to relax and observe. If you struggle against it, then you won't be seeing it clearly. If you try to stop it, kill it, suffocate it, repress it, you are actually reinforcing it. Work with the idea of not reacting to any reaction.

An Example from Gurdjieff

There is a story about Gurdjieff and Kathryn Hulme, one of the Ladies of the Rope.[52] She had a nickname – the Crocodile (*Krokodeel* as Gurdjieff pronounced it). The way she got the name was that she had flown from Europe to be in New York with Gurdjieff. At their meeting she wanted to share the experience she had when coming on the plane. There was a four-year-old girl one the plane who was flying alone to meet her parents in America. The little girl had a doll, and whenever there would be some difficulty on plane – this was in the 1940s – like it would hit some wind and the plane would rock, the adults would all be terrified. But the little girl would stroke the doll's head and say, "It's alright baby. Just relax. Everything will be fine."

Kathryn Hulme described this scene with sighs and total romanticism. She was saying, "Oh, that little girl was so mature; she was so grown up, and oh it was so wonderful watching her."

---

52 "Ladies of the Rope" – a group of women whom Gurdjieff worked with during the Second World War, so called because they were to consider themselves as tied together on a single rope, as they climbed this "mountain" of learning about and practicing the necessary work on self.

What she didn't realize was that Gurdjieff was tape recording the whole story. And, later on, in the evening, after dinner, Gurdjieff played the tape for everybody. Listening to the tape, it sounded completely absurd, completely empty, and completely full of emotion with no being, whatsoever!

Gurdjieff gave her the name "Crocodile" because in English there is this phrase "Crocodile tears," which is when somebody is overly sentimental about something, or totally romanticizes something. And when Kathryn heard the tape played, she was furious, and in the meeting she just couldn't do anything with her anger. "That's not fair, you didn't tell me that ... tape was on. You've embarrassed me in front of everybody. You cruel man," she said. She was really angry. It was only years later that she realized the full extent of her falseness; of her inflated romanticism. And then she was able to write about the experience with real clarity.

Gurdjieff had a phrase, "the horror of the situation." One of the ways I understand that is, we see ourselves in all of our brilliant, habitual mechanicality. Werner Erhard used to say that we are machines and we will always be machines. So, you can either be an unconscious machine or a conscious machine. If you are conscious, you're still a machine, but you can orient the machine in ways that are helpful, useful. If you are a conscious machine, you have choice. If you're an unconscious machine, you have no choice whatsoever, because even when we think we're choosing, our choosing is another form of having no choice, since the choice is already predetermined by our life script, our psychology, our mechanicality.

If you can look at your reactions without reacting to the reaction ... if you can get that far ... then you don't need any other instruction. Then, things take care of themselves.

It is difficult, I know. And, we all have to start somewhere. So, if you can't *not react* to the reaction, then don't react to the reaction to the reaction. Each step down the ladder it becomes easier to catch it. You catch it where you can and then you work up.

We Have the Answers

When shame is there, for example, obviously it doesn't do any good to pretend it's not, or deny it, or try to force it into a manageable little cage. Without judging the shame – in the sense of, "Oh, this is a handicap; Oh, why am I like this? Oh, I should be able to stand up for myself ..." or whatever – just look at it, directly, without compromise.

The thing itself reveals knowledge. You don't have to look for answers. All you have to do is look at what is arising without compromise. All the answers don't need to be found. We have all the answers. We just aren't getting the answers because we obscure them. When you look at the shame clearly, without compromise, then whatever information you need to be able to make things more workable, relative to your life and its unfolding, will be obvious, coincident to the uncompromised observation.

One of the key factors is no judgment. It is very simple, and difficult, because we are so used to "This is good," "This is bad," "This is right," "This is wrong," and sometimes the judgments are very subtle. But, this is what we want to work with – no judgment!

Obviously, if you take the average person and you give them a list of qualities, like shame, fear, anger, vanity, greed, affection, reverence, wonder, dignity ... pretty much everybody is going to say, "These are good," "These are bad," "These we want, these we don't want." It's a very natural response.

However, to deal with life directly, without compromise, we need to not be continually be dividing, dividing, dividing. And every judgment divides.

The ongoing aim is to realize the inherent unity of things. And, within that inherent unity, we want to realize the relative multiplicity, but always from the context of the reality of "unicity." So, all judgment, opinion, mental editorializing, all of that divides. Stop doing whatever divides. It's not a matter of doing something that unifies, it's a matter of stopping the doing of what divides. For example: *Shame arises. Okay, shame has arisen. Now what?* Just observe.

And, when you're observing without dividing, whatever information you need to work with the shame (or any other emotion) will be there. Because all the information we need about ourselves we already have. If we're in a profession, and that profession has a large body of data, like being a physicist or a doctor, then of course there is information we don't have; we need to study and research. But relative to ourselves, we have all the information necessary, we just have to allow that information into consciousness, which is pretty much what we're all experts at avoiding.

Fear, As It Is, Now

Just go one step at a time, which is to accept fear (or any other emotion) *as it is*. No expectation. No expectation of what it will get you, where it will lead ... nothing! No future. Just accept fear *now*, in this moment. That's the entire practice, the entire sadhana, the entire process. Then you'll see what happens.

If you accept fear in this moment, then, perhaps, there is something else in the next moment. But the next moment does not exist, and if you create it in your mind with your projections and your expectations, then it's literally impossible to accept this moment. Because you have created the next moment already! This moment can only be an effect of the next moment. You have to forget the next moment and accept this moment, here and now, totally, as if there is nothing else and never would be anything else.

One step at a time. Otherwise, if you've already got the second step planned out you can never take the next step. Do you follow that?

The funny thing (not in sense of comedic) is that often peoples' fears have no relationship to their present reality. Maybe the roots of that fear are really old, even archaic … maybe from childhood. Still, in our rational minds we *can* look at our lives and go, "Fear is arising, it is very strong, *and* clearly it has no relationship to the actual physical elements of my life." Then, we can have a sense that, as adults, we don't need to hold on to that fear.

Where fear of scarcity is concerned, probably the only thing lacking is the realization that we are not lacking anything. You start with observing the difference between the arising of the feeling and the arising of a reaction. Even if there is no ostensible logical reason for the reaction, it is still a reaction – in this case, a feeling of lacking. Then, use the clarity of your perception of that distinction to provoke practice, the practice of acceptance. The implication is, to ego, if I accept this feeling of "not enough" – whether of money, food, affection – I'm not going to have enough money, and not have enough food, or affection. But, after you've practiced that acceptance for some time you will get the idea that there is no connection between that fear and the reality. And that gives you a different doorway into the relationship. That's where you start.

Negative Emotions and Positive Emotions

Questioner: *Why is it that negative emotions seem to be more predominant than positive emotions?*
Lee: It doesn't matter why. If that's *what is*, that's *what is*. To be concerned with *why* rather than with acceptance is to intellectualize the whole thing and take it out of the domain of emotion and feeling. That doesn't mean we should not use our intellects – intellect is a great tool and is very useful. But we also tend to strategically use our intelligence to avoid dealing with emotions and feelings.

The way you find out why negative emotions tend to be predominant is to first accept things *as they are*. Inherent in complete acceptance is understanding, but acceptance is not a given aspect of intellectual clarity. Consequently, you could find out why, and your description could be true and accurate, but if you actually did find out why before you were able to accept, as it is, that there are negative emotions, then the probability of acceptance is diminished by a significant percentage.

The mind can understand very clearly with absolutely no connection to the rest of the body – which is most people's condition. When they go into any form of psychotherapy, they try to mentalize the whole thing: to study their dreams, study their unconscious and to come to the intellectual understanding, while denying the rest of the body, and the emotions. That's why bio-energetic forms of therapy are popular these days, because these forms start with the body and come to the mind later.

Work with acceptance. If fear comes first and then courage, in the moment in which there is only fear and the courage has not come yet, don't hold on to the courage. Just accept:

"There is only fear. Only fear." That's *what is*. And from there, if you accept, anything becomes possible.

Working With Judgments of Others

Questioner: *How can I work with my partner's judgments and anger toward me?*
Lee: First of all, he's who he is, you're who you are. You can't change him. Only *he* can change himself. And, relative to helping the other relieve their tensions, my experience is the best way to do this is from around the side, very unobtrusively. Through humor, and a kind of play. Because if we try to approach the tensions directly, usually we just provoke defensiveness and anger.

I don't know if you and your partner laugh a lot together, many partners don't, and it's a fantastic form of healing and harmony in any relationship. Instead of laughing at one another, you're enjoying something together.

Relative to your own practice, instead of trying to make room for his anger, you work with your own reaction to his judgment. Because trying to be silent and make room for his anger is more focused on him than on you. It is very common in relationship that the judgments are unfounded. People want to change one another, and in their frustration they have judgments that are not very accurate, but a function of their own frustration. If that is the case, then in fact you should have nothing to react to, because the person that he's got judgments on is not *you*.

So, work on your own state of being. With your self-confidence and self respect, you will develop the strength to realize that you don't need to react to other people's judgments. Those judgments come from other people, and they're never as bad as self-judgment. So, primarily work with what arises for you, and in that, there will be a greater spaciousness relative to your partner's manifestations.

On the other hand, sometimes our partner's judgments actually have some possibility of being useful to us, and we often refuse to accept any utility because of the tone with which the judgments are brought forth. When someone who is intimate with us is being critical of us, there may be absolutely nothing to the criticism. On the other hand, there may be something that we need to look at. So, it's useful to cultivate being able to make a distinction between the delivery of the criticism – which is often belittling, angry, demeaning, harsh – and the possibility that this person who is intimate with us and who knows us well is actually pointing to something. In which case, the tone doesn't matter because we're the one who is going to get value from the utility, not them.

CHAPTER 11

"Sit With It" or "Do Something Different"

When individuals have come to Lee distressed based in their difficulties in practicing with their minds and emotions, he has told some people to simply "do something different": to move the body, or even to say "shut the fuck up" to the mind. However, his overriding recommendation has been to stay present with what arises, to "sit with it [the disturbance] like a brick," as Werner Erhard said. In this series of essays Lee addresses a number of distinctions about how to work with the mind: including, at what point is it useful to "do something different," and whether or not this delays or diminishes the practice of simply being present to what is arising; to accepting "what is, as it is."

When it comes to working with emotions, Buddhist teacher Pema Chödrön suggests that you just sit with the emotional energy and let it pass.[53] Now there's a novel idea! How about that?

Of course some student is bound to say, "I have been 'sitting with it' for eight years … it hasn't passed yet." If that is the case you're not "sitting with it." If you're *really* sitting with it, it will pass, and relatively quickly.

---

53 Lee had been reading to the group from: Pema Chödrön, *No Time to Lose: A Timely Guide to the Way of the Bodhisattva*. Boston: Shambhala, 2005.

We are creatures of habit. With some women, their periods come every twenty-eight days like clockwork. Still, on the twenty-sixth day, when they start ripping people's heads off, and this has been going on for thirty years, they still don't get it. They still aren't able to say, "Oh, it's just my hormones," and sit with it, and see that two days later it passes. Instead, they go right ahead and rip people's heads off, like they're serious. Like those emotions are *real*. It's mind-boggling. (I talk like this so much that I'm sure I'm going to be a woman next lifetime. And I'm going to be pregnant a lot, so I know how it is to be ready to kill. Don't ever stand in the kitchen in the middle of the night and tell a pregnant woman she can't eat. Not if there are knives in the kitchen! The same with nursing mothers too.)

Even with the general, day-to-day run of horrible and beautiful emotions ... we can't just *sit* with them, *relax* with them, and let them pass. Instead, we need to blame somebody! Like in a support group, where one person blames, somebody else self-justifies, and at the end of the meeting everybody cries and hugs. But then, the same thing happens every meeting: one person blames, and then the person who is getting blamed self-justifies, and then starts to blame somebody else, because we all do this same thing. It's a great game, and everybody gets satisfied. Everybody takes the shit and then everybody defends themselves self-righteously, so then everybody is happy. Everybody gets to feel like they've had a good emotional bowel movement; a wonderful session of "standing up for their rights."

But, there is no law in the universe that says that when someone is blaming you, you have to self-justify. Still we do it anyway.

Pema Chödrön also says that we throw kerosene on the emotion so it will feel more real.[54] That's it! We are blaming somebody, and they're self-justifying (and oh, they're *sooo* good at it!), then we can really get on our blame trip and lay it on. We love it when someone self-justifies, because we get to throw kerosene on whatever emotion that we are putting out to the person who feels they've got to self-justify. It's great! Fabulous! If we can get cranked up, and really lay it on someone, then we feel that it's real! We feel like we're right. And then the person who is self-justifying gets to feel like their emotion is or was real! They can say: "Well, I have to defend myself. I have to bring clarity to the situation. I wanted the facts to be straight."

Why? What difference do the facts make? You have all been in relationships. Have you *ever* convinced your partner of the rightness of your position with facts? I don't mean something obvious, like your husband says, "How could you have spent all that money on that chair?" And you reply, "I spent nothing. Somebody gave it to me." I don't mean *that* kind of a fact. But, the subjective things, like:

"You were ignoring me this morning."

"No I wasn't, I said 'Good Morning.'"

"You did *not* say 'Good Morning.' I'm not deaf. I was sitting at the table and you did not say 'Good Morning.' So and so was also at the table. Let's ask her: 'Did he say Good Morning to me this morning?'"

"I don't know, I was busy trying to make words out of the O's in my cereal bowl."

The reality of things is that there is nothing you can count on. In spite of the fact that things are pretty reliable

---

54 *see* previous footnote

– like computers, and refrigerators, and cars (especially if we've kept them well-serviced), and of course our neuroses are pretty reliable (we know who's going to be late and who's going to be on time, and who is going to complain about the difficult traveling conditions, and who isn't – but essentially, all form is empty and all emptiness form. And, at any time, that realization could dawn. Some spontaneous event, something uncontrollable, could enter into the placidity of the predictability of our lives. And, under those circumstances, it helps to be able to see that circumstance as a circumstance that we can't control, and realize that we don't need to crank up the big guns and try to make it comfortable, predictable or controllable.

We don't always have to get confirmation from others or the world around us. If we're going through customs and the customs' agents or security person is in a bad mood and they snap at us, we don't have to get confirmation that we're a good person by excusing ourselves and smiling at them, making a joke, trying to lighten them up, getting them to be on our side. And, we don't have to get confirmation for the rightness of our integrity to be respected as a human being by going to security and complaining. We don't need legal recompense to make us feel like we've got our due, that justice has been served, that we've been confirmed because we've won this case. *We can just let it go.* Let it pass! Instead, we think, "I've been paying insurance; why not get a little back?"

The way we try to get "confirmed" is: we win a court case; we make somebody else pay for something. We don't just get confirmed by having someone smile at us and pat us on the back. We also don't get confirmed by winning no matter who else loses.

When we are able to stick with something that we can't control, something that has turned our world around, something that has shocked us, for good or bad (because wonderful things can do that also), by "sitting with" those things, then we can allow ourselves to be impacted by the reality of the spontaneousness of life, recognizing that control is death. Or, as Arnaud Desjardins would way, "Accepting *what is*, is life."

By saying, "No, no, no, no ... " – which is what "trying to control everything" is, because we can't control everything; it is an illusion – sooner or later *something* is going to come along that we can't control.

A Question About Control

Questioner: *I would just like to be absolutely clear.*
Lee: So would I.
Questioner: *Well, on this point of trying to control things, at least.*
Lee: I would just like to be clear about which came first, the chicken or the egg? Most other things don't bother me, but that ... *Not really.* I couldn't care less. It's irrelevant to me. I just thought it was something fun to say. I mean, who cares? Except some chicken philosophers! [*Laughter*]

When you feel the urge to try to control yourself, just relax, and observe, observe, observe. Observe the desire to control, and observe the way the information is being processed. Just pay attention. And if you are paying attention in the objective sense of that phrase, then knowledge will arise. You don't have to chase after it, and put things together.

Do Something Different

Somebody recently e-mailed me a relevant quote from Chögyam Trungpa, which says: "So, confusion and suffering has become an occupation."[55] It's true! We are willing to stick to confusion as our occupation and make it a habitual pattern of everyday life. In fact, that seems to be one of the main occupations of ego. Confusion provides a stable, familiar ground to sink into. It also provides a tremendous way of occupying ourselves. That seems to be one of the reasons there is a continual fear of giving up or surrendering.

Stepping into the open space of the meditative state of mind seems very irritating to us, because we are quite uncertain about how to handle that wakeful state. Therefore, we would rather run back to our own cell than be released from prison. Confusion and suffering have become an occupation, often quite a secure or delightful situation.

One of the distinctions about "doing something different" when the mind is disturbed has to do with the clarity of our self-observation. If we can understand that "confusion (and suffering) is our occupation" – if we are not in confusion about *that*; if we are not confused about our confusion and we are not suffering doubt about how we are creating suffering – then, at that point, we always do something different.

To "sit with" something *as it is*, to accept *what is, as it is*, is a means to an end. There is a point at which the means and the end are exactly the same, but in the beginning, when you begin to practice with accepting *what is, as it is, here and now*, it is a means to an end, the end being the realization of our

---

55 Trungpa, Chögyam, Rinpoche, *Transcending Madness: The Experience of The Six Bardos*, edited by Judith Lief, Boston: Shambhala, 1992, p. 202.

"profession" – that confusion and suffering are a profession (and sometimes a delightful profession).

When we have realized *that*, then we will also have realized, coincidentally, that *accepting what is as it is here and now* is not necessarily a passive state. Meaning that, even though we use the word "acceptance" (or we could even say "unconditional acceptance"), to accept unconditionally also means to accept our intelligence and our desire to be free of our suffering; to accept our wish to not only help others but help ourselves.

In all of those circumstances, what is demanded is to *act*, not to say "Okay, I have accepted," and then just go on stewing in our suffering. The whole point of "sitting with what is," "sitting with what is as a brick" is in order to realize something. Once we have realized what it is that that action of "sitting with it like a brick" is designed to produce in us, then we don't sit with suffering and bad financial circumstances and grief and jealousy and anger and fear. We don't sit with those things and let them turn us into babbling idiots. No, we *act*! And at that point an appropriate action is "do something different"!

We often think we can handle things – like mental input or emotional input – that we really can't handle. If we have a short burst of this input, that's generally okay. In such a situation we still have many options: we can go home; we can go on retreat; we can sit in front of our *puja* table [small devotional shrine]; we can sort ourselves into study; we can chant Yogi Ramsuratkumar's Name; we can call up a friend in the sangha, whatever, or we can drink some horrible-tasting tea, take some Chinese herbs; we purify and we burn off this stressful input. But if we have an extended period of time under such influences, like having to stay in a job that we really dislike, it's very difficult.

We "do something different" under two conditions: first, when it is simply a natural response to the circumstance we find ourselves in. In other words, we don't *have to* do something different as a motivated technology to change some negative state; rather, it's essentially a choice for health. But, in the beginning of practice, when we have no matrix for "sitting with it like a brick," if we try to, we're going to eat or drink ourselves into a stupor, or do something stupid, like hurting ourselves or getting into a car accident. Most of the time we are not going to make a choice for health. We're going to make a choice like, "Oh, okay, I'll go out drinking just this Wednesday, but, tomorrow is Thursday, so I won't drink tomorrow night." We will keep reinforcing the choices for lack of health.

So, the second point at which we "do something different" is when we can't do otherwise; when we are really weak and can't "sit with it like a brick." Instead, we can go out to eat; go to a mall; go to the right movie ... anything. We can start singing Broadway show tunes! We occupy our mind with something else besides whatever it is that is bearing down on us and creating suffering, misery, confusion, doubt, heartbreak, jealousy, anger or fear. Whatever it is!

And, when we have developed, through practice – but we have to *practice* in order to "develop through practice," remember that; if we don't practice, the phrase "when we develop strength through practice" does not apply to us – when we develop the strength to actually be able to "sit with" something, to be present with this screaming internal state, then ... But, ordinarily, we think that our unconscious is so demanding that we are sure we'll have a heart attack, that we'll die, that we'll blow up, that ... we don't know *what!* Which is exactly the thing: we never think about this "what."

When we are attempting to "sit with" something that we feel we can't bear, we don't stop to ask, "What's going to happen if I *just stay here* and feel this way?" Instead, we act – we get drunk, take some drugs, even natural drugs like fifteen vitamin-C tablets, although our rational mind knows that we can't digest that much vitamin C. We will digest three or four tabs and the rest we will just urinate out, but we take them anyway, because we are so desperate to fix whatever it is that needs fixing.

If we would really think to ourselves, "What *is* going to happen if I just stay here like this?" The answer always is *nothing*! I mean, maybe we'll kick the dog, okay. (But the dog probably deserves it anyway.)

We "do something different" when we don't have the matrix to "sit with something like a brick." It's a technique; it's clear; it's a method. It's just the way we are distracting ourselves, and we know it. It is just what we do with a child. When a child bangs himself and is crying, or is starting to get angry and crank up, we pick him up, run to another part of the room and stick some stuffed animal in his face, or a piece of chocolate, and within a couple of seconds his mind is changed, his attention is off whatever it was (which is why a lot of us have food disorders, because food works as a charm. Food is one of the best distractions for a child, and a lot of our parents used it. I too have used it on rare occasion.)

When we don't have the matrix to "sit with something like a brick," we treat our minds like babies, because they *are* just babies. But, we should be very clear that we are doing something different in order to distract our mind from what it is that is depressing it, frustrating it, and creating suffering. We simply want to put our mind on something else and get out of the suffering, and we can do this clearly, as an intentional technique, just to take a break; just to be able to stop and take a breath, and consider something from a different perspective.

Observe Yourself

When we practice to the point where we can "sit with something like a brick," then we do – and we observe: *What is this thing that I am observing telling me? What is it saying to me? What is this grief telling me? What is this jealousy telling me? What's the field, the network, in which this thing is the core of my attention?*

When we can "sit with something like a brick," we sit with it and we observe the whole complex that this is at the core of, in that moment. Like, "What *is* this?" Not necessarily "Where does it come from?" because that's not a terribly important question. If where it comes from happens to become apparent to us in our investigation, maybe it's useful, maybe not. But that's not the most important question. "What *is* this – this jealousy, this anger, this fear?" "What *is* this?" is the most important question.

With some people, for example, you can't shut them up; they never stop talking. But, put them in certain circumstances where they are absolutely petrified, and they can't get a sound out of their mouths. When we (or they) can "sit with *that*" – the fear, the embarrassment, the humiliation, whatever we are feeling – and our self-observation is about "What *is* this phenomena?" then something can happen.

Start self-observing on the grossest level – with the physical body. So, for instance, if you know that ordinarily you are loose and relaxed, and forward and gregarious, but in this particular circumstance you are completely paralyzed, observe what's going on in the physical body. Observe that your tongue is dry; that you could barely open your mouth; that your heart is beating fast; your face is flushed, and all the associated physical phenomena. Then, observe deeper and deeper and deeper.

When you *can* sit with something, then you don't do something different; you sit with it. Those of you who took the *est* course in the early days know that you had to fill out a card asking "Are you in therapy?" and if the answer was *yes* the second question was, "Are you being successful in that therapy?" What they meant by "success in therapy" was, are you seeing differences in your behavior. Success in therapy was when the results of the therapy were actually showing up in tangible, physical ways in your life. In the same way, when we are successful in our practice, the very fact that we have to "sit with something like a brick" is completely transcended, pierced, obviated. The same thing could come up again, but we would have no reaction. That's success! When we are successful, then, as noted earlier, we will do something different as a natural response to what is wanted and needed in the moment. We don't *have* to; it's not a technology; it is not something we will do intentionally, to change our mind, because our mind needs changing. Rather, it is simply a natural response to the circumstance.

Our other revelations or insights about the thing may be steps leading up to success (and there are lots of those), deepening insights into various dimensions of things, but these revelations are not the success itself. With success we completely get to the absolute root of the situation and the situation is not problematical anymore.

Practice is about building the matrix to "sit with" something, with the volcano of feeling, or the immensity of the emotion, whatever it is. Suppose you are sitting with grief of some kind and you want to just cry. Really cry hard, weep, sob. And suppose you are able to, in some ways, internalize the immensity of that, the cry of that sob. It might, as an experiment, be useful to cathect[56] instead of cathart,[57] to see what that produces. Because, ordinarily, in the vast majority of cases, when we hold something in, it forces the energy to coagulate instead of being spent out. And the coagulation of energy produces a magnification (or we could say an intensification) of the thing that we are observing.

Often, when we are trying to observe ourselves, we have trained ourselves over a lifetime to have fancy little ways of actually seeing something else, besides the thing that we think we are trying to see. When you force a kind of cathexis, and the thing intensifies, sometimes it shows itself to you.

But, some of us are highly skilled, and highly refined, and our powers of self-observation have been something that we have been actively practicing for more than half of our life. We may be observing internally, but still we remain cool, and totally in control. Sure, we are looking for something. But, we are looking *as part of* the very strategy that is going to compromise the "we" who is looking. How successful can that be? We have trained ourselves to make ongoing discoveries, that we call a deepening of self-knowledge, but in fact are just completely avoiding the core issue. And we are brilliant at it. We are perfect at it.

---

56 cathect: literally, to invest emotional energy *in* something. Commonly in Lee's work it means that emotional energy is simply not expressed.
57 cathart: to release emotional tension.

Cathexis and Catharsis

When you cathect, you intensify the thing. But, to cathect you have to be *out of control*, so you actually have something to cathect. As long as you are *in control*, there is nothing to cathect. So, when the immensity of the situation becomes such that you are out of control, you can cathart, which is to do the "mad thing," like beat on the pillow; do your "anger thing," get the anger out, breathe, scream, yell "Mommy, Daddy," and try to bring yourself back into balance. Or, if you have a matrix of practice so that you can "sit with it like a brick," you can cathect, which is like running the sun through a lens: all of a sudden instead you've got something that is going to burst into flames in an instant. Then, you can't avoid what it is that you'll be forced to see. Otherwise, if you cathart, if you beat the pillow or you sob, when you are done sobbing, the energy that was going to push you into territory that you have never been pushed into before is released and then you are back "in control," everything is cool.

 If you are really just "sitting with something like a brick," you won't have to decide whether you are at the end of the process of cathexis or not. You will just move on with what is arising *now*. You may be grateful and relieved for the lightening of the burden, that's natural, but essentially there will be very little need to investigate. We are all highly intelligent beings, so our associative faculties are not going to shut down; we are going to make associations anyway; so we don't have to investigate. The connections that are useful will be obvious, and the ones that aren't obvious aren't necessarily useful. We don't have to go digging for reason and meaning. When the experience of the moment is this kind of release, then we understand certain things and what we understand is all that we have to understand. If we start chasing after answers, the tendency would be to backtrack. Better to move forward.

Werner Erhard said, "Understanding is the booby prize." Understanding is for losers, because you understand with the mind, but you live with the being. You'll understand what you understand when you understand it, naturally, because you are intelligent. So, you don't have to try to understand. You have to perceive from a whole different viewpoint – the viewpoint of the context of reality, which of course is confusing and frustrating, and maddening and everything else. But, that's the demand. You view things from the context of reality, in which every contradiction ceases to be a contradiction because we see things holistically instead of partially.

Shifting the Obsession

Our response to something is always relative to the degree to which our mind is tamed and trained. The more trained the mind is, the more a recommendation like "do something else" will be completely effective. If when we find ourselves in a certain groove, we can switch grooves, *just like that*, this is very effective. If, however, the mind is not very well trained and we can't do that easily, then we have to use more stringent methods, like a shock – like a cold shower, or whatever.

Our particular response to mental distress will depend upon the level of our practice, literally. Even someone with a very strong practice is sometimes going to get blindsided by something that disturbs him. We just never know when a certain *something* is going to hit us; for instance, many people have become homeless because of an earthquake.

The senior recommendation is simply "be present with what arises." But, one has to practice *where one is*. So, we go and do something different when we have to. If we can remain present with what is arising without in any way harming anyone (not just physical harm; it could be psychological harm), or harming the space, or compromising our practice, then of course, that's what we do. Obviously, if we have a disturbed mind and somebody provokes us, and we have a pivotal point at which we can choose to get into it with that person or go do something different, to go do something different would probably avoid a tremendous amount of pain, emotional hurt, resentments, and who knows what else.

I want to emphasize the idea that to "do something different," in the ordinary way we talk about it, is just to *shift what your temporary obsession is*. Shift your obsession with suffering and occupy your mind with something more creative, more productive, more useful, whatever it might be. Singing show tunes is a great thing to do, another thing to do is clean the room, or answer all your mail, or pick up a book that you haven't finished or pull out your camera and dust it off and go to the camera shop and get into a conversation with the guy about what film you need to take certain pictures and go out and take a couple of rolls of film. It's amazing how many things each of us has that we could do that would completely shift our focus from some compulsion to suffer in the moment over something. Go through your clothes and start pulling out the things that you haven't worn in a year and probably won't and be really honest with yourself: "How much of this can I strip down? And how much do I really need. And, look at Yogi Ramsuratkumar. How much did *he* really need? Not much." Actually, make a conscious choice!

Emotions and the Will of God

To feel true emotions is not to have a boundary. Emotions are what they are, and anything can happen in relationship to them, not merely expression or suppression. In fact, I've been telling people a lot lately, when they ask, "What do I do with this emotion when it arises?" I say, "Do nothing."

We have this viewpoint that we have to do something with emotional energy. And that viewpoint is very narrow. We think that we either have to express it, in which case the energy goes away and it's not hot anymore, and then we can deal with it when it's cool; or suppress it, because somehow expressing it is bad, or not elegant. But, if we rest in the emotion *as it is*, which has all of space ... something else can happen.

From all of space, in the entire Universe this emotion has arisen. Realizing that, then we wouldn't have to express it or suppress it. We could just allow *space* to deal with it; space, we could say, is the Will of God. The Will of God will handle it. Then we don't have to do anything about it. Just let it be. Truly, let it be. Then we would not get psychosomatic illnesses because we were repressing all the time. Then, the energy would become useful energy instead of expressed energy (which does at least take the pressure off, like a steam valve). Or it might become repressed energy, which has to do something in the body, so it makes us sick in some way.

If you just "let it be," this emotional energy will not impair your functioning in any way. The only thing that can impair your functioning is doing something with the energy from the perspective of ego. If "letting it be" is allowing it to be the Will of God, how can it impair our functioning, unless it was necessary to impair our functioning? I can't think of an example of a spiritual master in which it was necessary for their functioning to be impaired, except in the case of the *mast*[58] who was talked about in one of Maher Baba's books. This man threw a stone at somebody and killed him. The *mast*'s functioning was impaired in a relative sense, because he was sent to prison, but not impaired in a real sense. He got out and just went back to the street corner where he always sat. All his old devotees came around and started sitting at his feet. It was business as usual.

One of my students observed recently that there are some real subtle lines between what we mean by "doing something" with an emotion, and what is just "letting it be." He found that giving the emotion state any thought whatsoever, whether it was a state of sadness, or sentimentality, or anything, even though he might not express the emotion outwardly to anyone else, was a vital form of "doing something" with that emotion that could impair the process. "Any thinking about it is like working on it, churning on it," he said, and he admitted that it was extremely hard for him not to get caught by this thinking. I definitely agree.

Making any distinctions about the content of our thoughts and emotions is a lot more difficult than always returning to the basic premise, which is, "Do nothing." Sometimes you may return to that premise and not be entirely effective with handling the emotional energy, but you should always give your attention to the context, not to making distinctions about the content. In terms of where you place your attention – always place your attention on context, which means just letting the emotion exist in space, *as it is*, or *what it is*.

Even when we are able to rest in the context there might still be some momentum behind the habit that will have to

---

58 *mast*: God-intoxicated madmen or women, typically mistaken by the culture to be insane.

play itself out. Eventually it will, but in the beginning it's still got a lot of momentum.

"Doing nothing" and the practice of enquiry are really exactly the same thing because when the practice of enquiry is true, there is "no one" doing it.

Keep Trying

A participant in a seminar in France was discouraged by the sense that he was making no progress in the emotional domain. He said, "I have the feeling that I have really practiced and really tried to apply everything that I know, but still the emotion is here, and it is not going away, what can I do?" Lee replied:

Try something you haven't tried. Not necessarily a different *form* but a different *mood*. You keep trying until it works. Now, if you're trying the wrong thing, and you get that feedback from somebody with the experience to give you that feedback,[59] then you try something different.

If the feedback you get is that the way you are describing the practice sounds clear, fine, then you just keep trying it.

If you do the same thing long enough, sooner or later you are going to hit it. And the first time it works it might not stick forever, but you'll know that it's worked, and you'll know that you're on the right track, so you keep trying it. And the second time it works, then you've got a little reinforcement, and a little bit more confidence, and you keep trying it. And at some point success becomes a

---

59 Lee is referring here to specific feedback or guidance from a spiritual teacher, or mentor, particularly in this case from one of the collaborators who work with students of Arnaud Desjardins.

little more consistent than random, and then you're really building momentum. That's the way you approach it.

If you find yourself getting discouraged, because you've tried everything and it's not working, then you apply exactly the same approach to the emotion of discouragement. That's the way you do it. Whatever arises in response to your feeling of: "This is not working; I've really tried everything; I don't understand why this is not working," you try relative to *that*. You apply the same response to whatever arises.

Stuck Energy

Questioner: When I can't express an emotion it gets just stuck. How can I ...?

Lee: What happens if you eat something that you don't digest well and you're stuck with it?

Questioner: I vomit.

Lee: Or you shit. So if the food is poisoned, you vomit; if the food is just difficult to digest, eventually it just comes out the other end – the ass, the butt, the rear end, the behind, the large cheeks. It's the same thing with emotions. If you're "impacted" (or constipated) because you can't express emotions, and you hold them, sooner or later you'll shit them out and then they'll go down the toilet instead of all over the people you live and work with. There's a saying in English, "Don't shit where you eat." And it's the same with the expression of emotions.

Questioner: You teach that it is possible to internalize emotions. What do you mean when you say someone can "observe the arising emotion"? Does that mean putting it somewhere it can't move?

Lee: No, putting it somewhere it cannot move is imprisoning it. That's different than interiorizing or internalizing it.

Questioner: *You repress the emotion?*

Lee: No. Repression, suppression and imprisonment is not interiorization. Suppression, repression and imprisonment are unhealthy. They can build up great charge and end up in explosion or breakdown, or something like that. Interiorization means to disengage from the identification with the emotion as being "you." Then the emotion arises, the emotion subsides, and you remain in equanimity. That's interiorization – to not be under the illusion that the emotion is the same as you. Is that clear in principle?

Questioner: *How and why do you do that?*

Lee: That's the question! That's why we enter the path, and why twenty years later we're still on the path. These things take time.

The way I teach, typically, is not by direct explanation. In principle, what happens when there is too much explanation is that the mind takes the explanation, monopolizes it and doesn't let it go anywhere else. Then it convinces us that we know completely, when all we know is mentally. We don't know in the body.

I teach by experience. In my company – meaning students who spend time in my company, not necessarily physically, but atmospherically in the school – people find that life will create specific circumstances that give them the possibility of experiencing what it is we have talked about or alluded to. Is that clear in principle?

To give too clear an explanation would actually be more of a detriment than a help in this situation. You have to trust the wisdom, the judgment and the blessing force of your teacher, who will set up life to give you the experiences necessary to understand the answers to your questions in a practical way – so that you can use them – not just intellectually. And that takes time. There is no fast way.

Hopefully, these remarks will have been some seeds planted that will begin to grow and blossom and, as time goes on, see roots start growing out of your ass. (I don't think I've been this crude in a seminar in fifteen years, at least. You all must be asking for it. It's not me!)

Part III

PRACTICE IN
A TOXIC WORLD

CHAPTER 12

Illness of Mind and Body

When I was teaching the Silva Method I used to hold the complete primacy of "mind over body."[60] I don't anymore. I think mind is a significant factor, but the toxicity of the world we live in cannot be understated. The physical body has been extremely sensitized in many people. When chickens eat toxic food their eggshells are thin and weak. Our "eggshells" are extremely weak and fragile. As a race we have been weakened – our entire immune systems, not just the physical immune system, have been weakened by the constant assault of toxicity. It's no longer simply a matter of illnesses being psychosomatic. The human race and, obviously, animal kingdoms are all in a state of transition, and toxicity is a very major player in the breakdown of physical health and mental health.

I am speaking of energetic toxins, also. In terms of the eight laws of the Buddha, we *can* pay attention to right thought, right speech, good company; and we don't want to underrate the effect that those things have on our overall state of being, on our mental and physical states. Negative thought

---

60 Silva Method: a psycho-physical method of personal growth and healing initiated by Jose Silva over fifty years ago.

absolutely affects, in a negative way, our mental, emotional and physical health. We should be watching what comes out of our mouths, first of all, and training ourselves to speak positively. You know the saying, "If you can't say it nicely don't say it at all."

Secondly, after we've developed a habit of right speech, then we work on right thought, because thoughts do have an effect. But, as I said before, even were we completely right-thinking, and right-speaking, and spending time in good company, the toxicity of the world is going to have its effect on a certain percentage of people. We are, generally speaking, a weakened and tremendously vulnerable species. And we're weakened by all the toxicity in the world including short-length waves, like microwave, X-ray, cell phones, the constant energetic pollution of our atmosphere by satellites, television, radio, cell phones, all of it. All of the wave technology – every wireless instrument, wireless computer, wireless everything else – can't help but affect the body, and the mind!

If you were a highly trained yogi, you might be able to buffer yourself from those things, but *we* can't completely buffer ourselves from them. So, we simply work with right thought and right speech, which we should take seriously as practices. And, I might even suggest that the more emotionally bonded you are with who it is you're speaking negatively about, the more negative the effect. If you speak negatively about George Bush, you don't know him; he doesn't mean shit to you. But if you speak negatively about your brother or sister, or your mother or father, or one of your sangha-mates whom you're bonded to, that has a big charge; primarily on you, and more subtly on the person you are speaking about.

Toxic Body/Toxic Mind

Chögyam Trungpa said that television was the worst invention ever made, and that it destroyed people's minds, children's minds. Obviously, the virtual realities that we're dealing with now are a hundred times worse than television.

I don't think there is any way around using computers, but for people who have small children in my community I recommend that, under no circumstances, unless required by law, should children have a computer before age fourteen. To me, anything else is criminal.

Many of us have said, "Television, *boo, boo!*" but then with computers and the Internet we vie with one another to see who is going to get their child a computer first so that they can "kill themselves" with this technology even more than television would. In schools now they're training children from probably first grade up to use computers. Their rationale? Well, "There are too many dissenters in this great country of ours. We need to get them in line." And boy, is *that* a way to do it, by getting them *on*-line. People who are raised on computers are completely malleable, except for the few heretics and rebels who will fight against the system. And they'll probably be hunted down, like other dissenters in science-fiction movies, in one way or another. Maybe not in the next ten years, but give it thirty, forty, fifty years.

We now have generations of young people raised on toxic food, and a toxic environment, and television and media. How can they be healthy? They are also probably experiencing some elements of nihilism, fear of the future, and concern for their families and their well being. The way children are pushed in school I think there's some concern among young people about whether they're going to be able to compete in the world with all of these genius robots who are going to law school and becoming doctors and everything else. There are very real concerns that young people have and have had in the last thirty or forty years.

We live in a completely toxic world in which children are becoming more and more habitually addicted to poisonous behavior. I don't mean criminal behavior, I mean poisonous behavior and poisonous substances, and I don't mean marijuana. I mean cookies and junk food and burritos laced with preservatives, and Taco Bell and Wendy's and Subway, and all of those "good places" to eat. I don't think teen suicide is a simple issue. I think that it's impossible to separate, in a holistic sense, the complete toxification of a child's mind and body. Body chemistry is so fucked up from the way it's supposed to be naturally, and maybe in a hundred years, given Darwin's evolutionary theory, we will adjust. And maybe in a hundred years we'll be able to eat anything and our bodies will have adapted to chemical diets. But, right now, I don't think we can take the complete toxification that children experience away from their mental and emotional states. It's a very complicated issue.

Depression

In working with depression the bottom line is that we do the best we can. If we can't hold steady, we go to the next level, which is the same thing as moving from naturopathic treatment to allopathic treatment. There is a distinction between psychological depression and spiritual depression and it's important not to mistake one for the other. With psychological depression, if it's necessary to treat it with antidepressants you do. Spiritual depression would be a kind of profound remorse based on seeing reality as it is, and either realizing your failure to practice in the past, or realizing your unwillingness to practice in the present. That kind of shock would create what I would call spiritual depression. Your commitment to the path may be unquestionable, but your realization of your own unnecessary failures relative to the path can creates a temporary but very deep remorse. Under that circumstance of depression created by remorse, to mask or buffer yourself against that insight and realization is completely counterproductive to progression in practice. You would want to allow the "burn" of the remorse to actually push you.

Chögyam Trungpa Rinpoche called all therapeutic modalities, including therapeutic modalities supposedly based on Buddhist principles, "the great path of discovering *me*." He was not in favor of any of them, but I'm sure he allowed people to participate in therapy because he was frustrated with their unwillingness to practice at the level that he offered.

Trungpa Rinpoche was very blunt about it – if you're going to use your mind, why waste it trying to discover the sources of your psychological imbalance. Simply take the psychological imbalance and use it as "food," as fuel for work. He was highly critical of all this going back into your childhood and finding out what happened and why you feel the way you feel. And now, of course, Chögyam Trungpa Rinpoche is being heralded as a great teacher, whereas during his lifetime he was verily reviled. Now he is hailed, not by everyone, but by sources that completely refused to acknowledge him during his lifetime. Today these same sources are acknowledging that he made a unique contribution to Buddhism in the West and that nobody else could have done it but him ... and on and on. Anyway, he's somebody to listen to.

If you're going to use your mind, why not use your mind to practice instead of to obsess about something that you're going to leave behind when you die, something that earns you no good karma or merit, something that's just a complete self-machination? Obviously the tricky part is how to tell which condition is "psychological depression" and which is "spiritual depression." One would suppose that one would recognize spiritual depression because of the focus of the thought process relative to what's depressing. But, I wouldn't jump to any quick conclusions. I wouldn't be too quick to label the depression as one or the other, no matter who gives you feedback. Whether it's a spiritual teacher or a psychologist who gives you feedback, you're going to get different feedback.

As Chögyam Trungpa Rinpoche suggests, allow your psychology to show you how unnecessary it is to dwell in the past traumas. If recalling and working with a childhood trauma can be used to clarify the insubstantiality of psychological phenomena, therein lies great value. If, on the other hand, it mires you more deeply in that domain by re-traumatizing, then it's useless work and even counterproductive. You use the pain of any situation to give you a glimpse of the *shunyata* (the emptiness) of whatever it is; use the pain to give a bigger remembering than you're seeing or feeling.

If you match any psychological reference against the dharma, you will come up with the validity of dharma and the insubstantiality of the psychological reference. The study of dharma is the matrix that you stand in, in order to use personal and psychological identifications as inspirations to practice.

Working With the Past

Student: *Suppose you have a memory of an emotional experience of your mother slapping you across a room. Are you suggesting that we remember that and consider that this was our karmic destiny in that moment? Are you saying to realize that there were other factors involved, so we don't get hooked into blame in the same way?*

Lee: Not getting involved in blame is the result, not the method. The method is: you remember the incident and you say to yourself something like, "Well where is it now?" Then you realize, "Okay it's nowhere now; so what was it then? Well, I was a child, I was very vulnerable then. And now?"

That's the way you continue to reference a situation until you see that everything in the past is completely insubstantial and it doesn't exist anymore, except in our memory and in our willingness to continue to revivify it.

Therapeutic Help

What Chögyam Trungpa Rinpoche would say is that you don't wall off any memory as if it is substantial, as if you're going to put it somewhere where it can't affect you. No. You want to pierce the entire illusion of that event or experience as substantial. Keep bouncing against (that is, "working with") the understanding that the entire illusion is insubstantial. Then, when you're in a situation in which a certain little push (like some therapeutic help) is needed, you take the push, psychologically speaking, therapeutically speaking. As long as in "taking the push" or "entering the process" you understand that you're trying to get some immediate help, for an immediate situation, and that you're not basing your hopes on enlightenment on that therapeutic process.

Within our community, the intention is to develop a context in which people who need a push in some area, or a regression in some area, or whatever they need, can be offered that, in the context of practice. Even if the person gets distracted, the therapist doesn't, and is able to keep the person focused on the right priority without denying any immediate help that can be very useful.

If you make an impassioned enough and genuine appeal to the guru and the lineage, then it gets taken care of, in the way that it needs to get taken care of, which is not always pleasant. You might make the appeal in a state of health and clarity, and then when you get slapped around a little bit, you might say, "Hey, I didn't think it was going to be like this!"

It's more likely that, when these primal states arise, if those states are arising as a result of a supplication made to the guru and the lineage, that they are purificatory. And, one would assume that, when such states come up we have the skills to work through them, not a hundred percent, perhaps, but pretty much.

There's a difference between being catapulted into primal states through a trauma that is the catalyst – a catalyst which the guru and the lineage have used to get us "there," so that the vulnerability that we experience when we're "there" is receptive to the purificatory influence and the blessing force of the guru and the lineage; as opposed to the trauma just being some random event, an accident, or even karmic feedback.

We never know how long it's going to take, or when breakthroughs are going to happen.

Slaves to Primal Emotions

Ordinarily we are slaves to our primal emotions. Things happen to us and we make decision based on that. "I'm bad, I'm talented, I'm stupid," like that, and for the rest of our lives we function in a way that confirms that original decision.

I was just reading about anorexia, and how a fair number of Christian saints in the Middle Ages were actually anorexic, because the definition of sanctity included a complete hatred of the body. It was a perfect circumstance to be considered very saintly instead of being considered very sick. The basis of anorexia, according to this book, is a feeling of never being good enough. That gets translated into never being thin enough. This is a decision that is made as an infant based on some stimuli in the environment. Maybe our father says to us, "I hate fat women; there's nothing worse than fat women," and we're three years old and something clicks. We spend the rest of our lives, no matter what our objective body image is, wanting our father to love us. We don't feel that he does, so we get thinner and thinner. It's a standard scenario based on a primal decision.

We can try to change those primal imperatives by efforts of will, and occasionally we can be successful at that, but ordinarily we won't be. Our unconscious will always find some way of sabotaging the change. We have a failure mechanism and we take a positive thinking course. We decide we're going to buckle down and think hard and make more money. And we actually start making more money, but some disaster always happens that takes all our financial reserves. We sabotage ourselves – our house burns down, we wreck our car. Something always happens.

Often primal decisions have to do with our emotional state, which is much subtler. "I'm only going to be happy (or unhappy) when these conditions are met," or "I'm only going to be full of pride or vanity when these conditions are met." It makes no sense. I'm sure you've all seen a man with a really grossly obvious, cheap hairpiece looking in the mirror like no one can see him being completely vain, when actually the hairpiece makes him look like a clown. Or a sixty-five-year-old woman who is dressing like a sixteen-year-old, walking along looking in the mirror, imagining that she actually looks like a sixteen-year-old. Anyone looking at that from the outside wonders, "How can that person not see?"

The point is that our manifestations are not spontaneous, and part of the transformational process, which is accepting ourselves as we are, doesn't eliminate those qualities. They don't go away; they become qualities that serve our lives but don't define our lives. If rage can protect our children, instead of saying, "Rage is bad and I shouldn't manifest rage, I should have equanimity," there it is and it gets used.

So when we accept what is as it is, without judgment, without opinion, it alters the mechanism of the fear, anger or happiness. The body in its total complexity – not separated into psychology, personality, mind, emotion, the astral body, the ethereal body and all this business – begins to function holistically when we accept what is. The body naturally and instinctually produces what is of value in any given circumstance; what is not of value the body doesn't animate. If fear is valuable, fear arises. If fear isn't valuable, fear doesn't arise.[61]

---

61 Young, M. *As It Is, A Year on the Road With a Tantric Teacher*. Prescott, Arizona: Hohm Press, 2000, pp. 499-500

CHAPTER 13

Standing Firm in the Dharma

A professor from Ohio State University wrote a book recently using factual data to substantiate his premise that the probability that any American citizen will get killed in America by a terrorist is so small as to be statistically negligible. Essentially, he is saying that the entire terrorist "thing" is trumped up in order to get the American people to hand over their complete power and authority to the government.

The mind is happy to bury its head in the sand as long as it can be minimally convinced that it's got some sanctuary. If we can be convinced that terrorists are more dangerous to us than our own government, then of course we'll support our own government to almost any length to protect us from terrorists.

In the U.S., one of the directions we are moving in is that all of our money is being spent to protect us from illusions, instead of the money going to education and care for people. This is at the source of the problem to begin with. You can't expect high school students to all of a sudden get a conscience when they've been raised since the time they were little babies, since the time they could understand language, to be afraid of those "nasty Muslims," those "nasty French," and anybody else who is not an American ally; or to be afraid of those "nasty niggers," "nasty kikes," and "nasty gays" ... whoever and whatever the majority of the American populace tells their children to be afraid of.

The longer we move in that direction, the more the media will assault our minds. For example, if you walk into a mall, you probably don't look at every display in every store window; if you flip through a magazine, you probably don't stop and pay attention to every ad or read every article. But, we know from studies in hypnosis and regression that the mind sees and hears and smells *everything*. So, the more there is an investment in society being a certain way, on the part of those who have the authority and the power to make that investment, we will be inundated by that "certain way" message. And, most of the time, we won't be paying conscious attention to that message, because most of the time that message is going to be hidden in articles, in photographs, in ads, or in the music in malls. We know that technology is presently available to get people to be in the mood to shop, depending upon what sub-auditory sounds or vibrations are being broadcast in the mall. The fact that a report about the experimenting with these things recently got into a newspaper is a miracle. Still, one newspaper article is a drop-in-the-pan cry of outrage, which quickly died. Nobody is doing anything about it, except for a few crank groups.

The reality of the situation in the world today is beyond our ability to believe! Not beyond our imagination, but beyond our ability to believe. Hearing about such things, as the sex trade in young children, we may say, "Oh, my God!" But our minds will immediately say, "That's impossible. That is just too far out, too horrible, too cruel, too ... whatever."

We, spiritual students, are attempting to be a part of the movement that Paramahansa Yogananda talked about when he was alive; a movement toward small groups of devoted disciples bonded together and struggling to survive through the complete breakdown of the world as we know it. He talked about going out into the woods and remaining invisible.

Here, we are finding ourselves literally assaulted by, in many cases, sub-sensory information, and one of things that we are supposed to be doing is to make conscious decisions.

We have a pretty significant responsibility. We are constantly called upon to make choices about our children, about all their lives, and to make decisions about the livelihood that we seek. On what do we base the decisions we are making?

To guard our practice (and in guarding our practice to guard the authenticity of this transmission through our lives and the lives of our children and grandchildren, and so on), to keep this lineage alive, is to not fall prey to the direction in which this world is going. We must not make decisions based on what the media is feeding us all day long and all night long. And nobody can do that for us. People can help us heal, can give us medicine, advice, many forms of help, but nobody can manage our minds for us.

Knowing What Is

The first step to awareness is knowing the direction the world is going in, and how that whole field of energy is being fed and maintained and multiplied and nurtured. If somebody says, "The world is so materialistic, and we're losing our values," most of us would agree. We understand that. But there is a difference between agreeing with that viewpoint because we know it's true, and knowing it.

The methodology of seducing entire populations is no mystery – you buy up all the media. You allow the media to maintain the names of things that people are used to, like Christianity did with the mystery religions when they first took over. You let people get used to the idea that things are changing, and slowly you just co-opt, until eventually you've completely co-opted the whole thing, and nobody even knows that there is a trace left of the old religion. Then you've got the whole population. If you just move in, changing everything and expecting the population to jump on the bandwagon, they won't, because they won't use their intelligence, even if you've got a better religion and free healthcare with the doctor of your choice! Even then you won't jump on the bandwagon if it's too radically different from what you are used to. The way entire populations are subverted is slowly, from underground, or sideways, until they are so used to the competitive images, that even when these images start to become more common than the old images, people don't mind, and then ...*Gone!*

It's up to us to not fall prey, in the decisions that we make, to this kind of subversion. Anybody who becomes a part of this lineage is personally responsible to see that the decisions we make are decisions that stand for clarity, and the integrity of right action, right thought, right meditation, good company, the just laws of the Buddha. And that is a very difficult thing to do because we are constantly being seduced by media that knows how to address our deepest psychological weak spots, and doesn't have to come out and say what they want. They can use images and symbols to make us dance to their tune, without actually saying anything, so that our minds are not even involved.

We have to get our minds involved. We have to be attentive if we want to maintain the integrity of this path and lineage over a long period of time. It is our immediate responsibility to recognize what is happening in the world and not just despair as a philosophical statement of intention, but to actually be able to stand in the day-to-day decisions that we make. Many times it is the best of bad choices, as in politics ... a lot of people are voting *against* something rather than *for* something.

We are making decisions all the time — about what we eat, what we read, what movies we see. It is our responsibility to pay attention to the basis on which we make decisions as if there were no separation between our practice and our dharma and anything that has to do with our lives: public school, children, profession, travel, wherever we find ourselves, even shopping in WalMart. There shouldn't be any separation, but we haven't completely come to terms with our unconscious yet.

We need to affirm to ourselves, "Everything that my life is about, from the most mundane (like picking up clothing at Sears), to sitting for meditation in the morning, is not separate from the holistic process of having found my path, my guru, and having begun to practice in very particular ways. The decisions we make should be based on dharma, not on the materialistic momentum that culture and society has been inundating us with for years.

We recently saw a new John Lennon documentary [*The U.S. vs. John Lennon*, 2006]. It was very touching and tender, and very depressing, in a way. Because, whatever the documentary was telling us to be aware of is already so far beyond where it was when John Lennon was alive. It is almost like that documentary, politically and socially, is irrelevant, because we are so beyond that state of fascism. I suppose every drop in the bucket in a useful drop; every straw on the camel's back is a useful straw; because we never know which is going to be the final straw!

It weighs on us to not be assuming, even unconsciously, that there is some part of our lives that has nothing to do with our involvement on the path. Because *everything about our lives* – how we advise our brothers and sisters, aunts and uncles and friends (many of you have had family call up in some kind of crisis and ask your advice) – is involved. Do we advise family and friends based on what we think to be an economic reality, or based on dharma? Of course economic reality and dharma are not separate either; there is dharma that applies to economic reality. How do we become so rooted, so immersed in dharma, that dharma permeates?

It is our personal responsibility to unify our lives to the degree that where we live, eat, breathe, move and think, as devotees, is rooted in the path, influenced and educated in dharma, and strengthened by our practice, our devotion and our faith.

The Last Word – Just be Kind

Questioner: Could you explain how transformation is being lived in this body, since it's in the present, here and now?
Lee: No, actually, I can't. Well, I can talk about it, but I can't explain it. Is there any more to your question?
Questioner: I ask this because of all the illusions and imaginations we can have about transformation. I would like to know what I could maybe do, because that's what I want – transformation.
Lee: You don't have to label your illusions to be able to live life in reality or truth. How you act is the first thing – that is, with kindness, generosity, compassion, dignity, respect, the ability to extract joy from life when there is joy, and sorrow from life when there is sorrow – regardless of what goes on internally. We can call that discernment, or discrimination.

Academically speaking, if through your entire life you acted with impeccable integrity – serving others, and blessing the universe through the clarity of your behavior – it wouldn't matter what you were thinking or what you were doing interiorly. If you died having never indulged the negative obsessions of ego – the anger, the greed, the violence, the cruelty, the pettiness, whatever – then you would be considered a great saint (and probably you would be).

One of the problems in dealing with the mind is that we've got to deal with the mind! If we didn't deal with it at all, and simply acted in a way that was consistently reliable – with kindness, generosity, compassion, dignity, and so on – we might not feel enlightened, but we would *be* enlightened, at least as good as enlightened, and maybe even better, in fact.

A Teaching Beyond the Mind

by Regina Sara Ryan

In his lectures and seminars, Dr. Robert Svoboda, the noted Hindu scholar and author, will often warn his listeners – after he's spent hours describing some intricate technology for karmic dissolution or alchemical transformation – that there is another way to better make use of all the material he has just shared. He may say something like this: "Basically, you can spend years perfecting all of this, *or* you can drop whatever you're doing right now, and run to the Feet of Lord Shiva, and bow down saying, 'Oh Lord, please accept me as your humble servant.'"

This remark generally startles Dr. Svoboda's listeners. On the three occasions when I've witnessed it, I see that some participants laugh nervously, some breathe a sigh of relief, some put down their pens for a moment, eyes wide, resting from the avid note taking they have been engaged in. A cloud lifts from the room. A truth settles. Somehow, it seems to me, we all know that this remark reflects a deeper level of truth; one that undermines all our grasping for insight and knowledge and mastery. In the act of bowing down, the

Universe is set right again. In the act of invoking the Lord (Shiva in this case), we have acknowledged our own helplessness and simultaneously relieved ourselves of a burden that lies heavily on our shoulders – that of maintaining the illusion of separation.

In the mood of Robert Svoboda's example, then, this Afterword, 'A *Teaching Beyond Mind*, is offered as a reminder to readers. My thesis here is that Lee Lozowick's teaching about mind and emotions, which you have read and perhaps wrestled with in the previous pages, is best concluded with a caveat similar to that of Dr. Svoboda's. In my words, "You can spend years working on technologies of practice – observing the mind, dealing with obsessions, delving to the root of your addictions, practicing non-reactivity or the non-expression of negative emotions, and so on. Or, you can drop whatever you are doing right now, and at every opportunity possible, especially the moments when your mind and emotions are flailing out of control, and *run* to the feet of the Lord (your *ishtaa devata*, your guru, or in Lee's case, the feet of Yogi Ramsuratkumar), and bow down saying: 'Oh Lord, consume this mind, consume these emotions, and turn all things to good in your service." Or whatever words work for you!

I dare to propose that, heeding this advice, you would then be practicing more in line with the way Lee Lozowick himself practices. My bold proposal comes as a result of living with and studying Lee's teachings on the subject of mind and emotions, specifically, for a long time. During the process of compiling the transcripts and editing the material for this book – a work that stretched out for over two years – I took a few weeks off for an extended retreat. Study material for this period consisted of one Buddhist text on the subject of mind, together with the second volume of Lee's poetry, *Gasping for Air in a Vacuum – Poems and Prayers to Yogi Ramsuratkumar.*

At the time of this retreat, I was struggling with this current book project. *Feast or Famine* was still a far distant goal. For all the hundreds of hours of transcripts that I had to work with – some of the most relevant of which you have just read in this book – I was far from satisfied that I had adequately represented Lee's teaching on mind and emotions. Something was missing – something which I hoped to generate by asking Lee more specific questions after my return from the solitude of the desert experience. Three days into the retreat, however, the answer to what was missing was apparent to me.

As part of retreat practice, I was reading dozens of Lee's poems every day – these prayers and testimonies of praise written to his Father, Yogi Ramsuratkumar, since 1983. Because of my current obsession with his teaching on mind, I was drawn to a line here or there where Lee mentioned his own mind – calling it the "monkey mind," or the "foolish mind," or even the "dog-donkey mind." The more I read, the more I was astounded that the poetry actually contained consistent references to mind. And, moreover, these references, when noted and studied, revealed a level of teaching about the subject of mind and emotions that, while perhaps obviously implicit in Lee's relationship to life and to his master, Yogi Ramsuratkumar, are nonetheless rarely elaborated in his usual seminar talks in France, or in sessions of answering student questions at his ashram in Arizona. It occurred to me that, because his formal teaching sessions are so often driven by the questions of his students, that I must look elsewhere to learn more about his own relationship to "the" mind – and "his" mind in particular.

Ultimately, I found that his poetry honored a relationship to God in which Lee's own mind was no longer held as "his." Rather, he frequently astonished himself with the fact that, together with his speech and the works of his hands, his heart and mind have long been surrendered to the feet of his master, Yogi Ramsuratkumar. (This surrendering itself being the work of Yogi Ramsuratkumar, not Lee's own, he admits.) From Lee's perspective, therefore, nothing that mind creates has any personal implications; and therefore no emotional responses are relevant.

Again, in my words, what seemed to matter to Lee was his intention of worship and his ongoing yes to surrender. Whether his worship and adoration looked splendid or stumbling, it was no longer his effort that accomplished it. He no longer identified with the mind – his mind – even if it still annoyed, distracted and even captivated him for longer or shorter periods of time. Instead, everything – every thought, every arising emotion, every word out of his mouth, every dream, goal, wish, every tiny gesture – was a cue to remembrance, an opportunity for praise, and a gift to offer back to his guru, Yogi Ramsuratkumar, the One in whom Lee accessed the source of All. With neither humility nor grandiosity, Lee admits that, in his experience, there is no longer any separate one to generate thought or emotion.

These insights about Lee's relationship to mind and its connection to the essence of his relationship to his master, excited me, needless to say. And I spent the remaining weeks of my retreat finding more and more examples of this phenomenon. Returning to Lee's ashram afterward, I presented my discoveries to him, asking him to comment publicly about this aspect of his teaching. At last,

I thought, I would have a concluding piece for the book; a chapter that would set all the rest in perspective, and a final gift to readers.

Lee surprised me again, however. "You write it," he said, almost off-handedly, without a smile or a frown. I almost protested, but bit my lip. Instead, I clarified. "You want *me* to write a chapter in the book – your book – in which I point to another level of your teaching – one which is not found in ordinary conversations or explications?" "Sure," he said, and smiled.

And so, a year later, as the publication deadline for *Feast or Famine* was fast approaching, I finally sat down to put it all together.

Mind in the Poetry

Everything that I found in Lee's poetry relative to mind and emotions was basically resonant with tenets that have long characterized his Work. He began his teaching asking his followers to assert "Just This," the means by which one falls into complete alignment with "what is, as it is, here and now." His poetry reflects this, consistently.

His teaching progressed to the revelation that "the only grace is loving God," in which he acknowledged humanity's complete and utter helplessness and dependence upon the Will of God. His poems are full of this on-going revelation.

And finally, Lee gave his devotees the directive to chant the Name of Yogi Ramsuratkumar, in all things, under every circumstance. Keeping God as our focus, Lee says again and again, in his poems and prayers, all things fall into place. And this teaching echoes the teaching of "Father is All" that was so radically lived by Yogi Ramsuratkumar.

To make a long story very short, Lee's poetry demonstrates and celebrates that we don't have to have an elaborate dharma, a complicated series of practices, and a technology for mastery of the mind. There is, in fact, another way. The job is simply to acknowledge our own helplessness, and turn everything over to the Lord. Lee has run to the feet of Yogi Ramsuratkumar and bowed down. The same possibility exists for any of us.

In fact, in his poetry Lee makes direct reference to deliberately turning his back on most traditional methodologies that attempt to elaborate mind-essence. He honestly doesn't much care anymore about the practice of taming or training the mind from these conventional perspectives. If a "training" or a "stabilizing" is in store, it is achieved through his constant practice of turning everything over to His Father. The Name of Yogi Ramsuratkumar dissolves or obliterates mind. Period. Then, the Divine alone moves, with the human psycho-physical complex providing the vehicle.

I believe that Lee's practice of writing almost daily poetry of praise and prayer has been his means of stabilizing in this practice of turning all over to his Father. With everyone who approaches him, moreover, Lee urges the repetition of the Name of Yogi Ramsuratkumar, which is, in effect, his way of sharing his own mind-training with us.

Two Stages in Work with Mind

The different levels of work with mind and emotions that I refer to here have been well described by other mystics throughout the ages. In the last century, Sri Aurobindo noted a two-stage process of spiritual unfoldment in his book, *The Synthesis of Yoga*. He wrote:

First, there will be the personal endeavor of the human being, as soon as he becomes aware by his soul, mind, heart of this divine possibility and turns towards it as the true object of life, to prepare himself for it and to get rid of all in him that belongs to a lower working, of all that stands in the way of his opening to the spiritual truth and its power ...[62]

This first stage – the time of "personal endeavor" – is the stage in which we, the readers of this book, are presently engaged in practice. It is in this stage that we are most concerned to do the right thing. It is in this stage that we come to the teacher or master asking for help – for practices or strategies to deal with the wild mind and the emotions that obsess us. We have certainly recognized "a divine possibility," and we know that we must be prepared, must "get rid" of what belongs to "a lower working."

And so, this book *Feast or Famine* can serve as a handbook to this first stage of spiritual work. Drawn from Lee's discussions for over thirty years, we find that he has been charting the course that must be taken when the mind is untamed; when the emotions are raging out of the control; when we are caught in confusion, doubt and fear. He has pointed out to us, over and over, how to regain some equilibrium. He has reminded us to never forget our purpose. Only then, as we find echoed in the words of Sri Aurobindo, are we able to enter into the second stage of this Yoga.

The second stage of the Yoga will therefore be a persistent giving up of all the action of the nature

---

62 Aurobindo, Sri, *The Synthesis of Yoga*, Part IV, Vol. 21, Sri Aurobindo Birth Centenary Library, Pondicherry: Sri Aurobindo Ashram, 1972, p. 592

into the hands of this great Power, a substitu-
tion of its influence, possession and working for
the personal effort, until the Divine to whom we
aspire becomes the direct master of the Yoga and
effects the entire spiritual and ideal conversion of
the being.[63]

Lee's guidance of his students in this second stage of
the Yoga – the "persistent giving up of all action … into the
hands of this great Power" – while a definite undercurrent
of his more explicit teachings – is found with crystal clarity
on every page of poetry he writes to Yogi Ramsuratkumar.
We find here, moreover, that Lee's "giving up" is not marked
by any efforting. Instead, his giving up is actually identical
to a continual paean of praise, in which everything becomes
food for the fire of adoration.

Lee's poetry orients himself (and other lovers of God,
along with him) in the practice of Remembrance; the
practice of calling upon the Divine Name; the practice
of recognizing his own helplessness, and the practice of
patiently awaiting the infusion of Divine Benediction. In
fact, I believe that precisely because this second stage is so
integral to his own core teaching, Lee can not be pinned
down to one linear practice path relative to the first stage.
I assert that he appears to live in the second stage. And,
beyond that, in the realm characterized by "entire spiritual and ideal conversion," that is, subsumed by the life of
Yogi Ramsuratkumar. Is it any wonder that he is less than
enthusiastic, after thirty years of repetitive instruction, to
deal again and again with the basics?

---

63 Aurobindo, ibid.

Legitimizing the Illegitimate: A Warning

The writer Lawrence Shainberg (*Memories of Amnesia: A Novel*, and *Ambivalent Zen*) had numerous personal contacts with Samuel Becket, the Nobel Prize-winning playwright noted for his revolutionary vision and his ability to communicate absurdity, a characteristic of life in the here and now. In writing about Becket's work, Shainberg felt a twinge of conscience about explaining things. He noted the great writer's "… devotion to the immediate and the concrete, the Truth which becomes less True if made an object of description, *the Being which form excludes*."[64]

This attempt to interpret the work of an artist by making it "an object of description," particularly when it comes to overlaying meaning on an expression of the non-linear, has long been criticized by artists of all types. And, a similar hesitancy clouds my approach to Lee Lozowick's teaching. While I am clear that Lee intends to rouse his listeners from the sleep of identification with mind and emotions, I am not clear at all that my explicating of anything serves his purpose. With this in view, then, the reader is urged to read Lee's own words, first and foremost. To be moved by them, shocked by them, or bored by them, as the case may be, and only secondarily to rely upon commentaries, such as this one.

"Translation takes place in a dusk or twilight where two different and unequal worlds meet and occasionally collide," says the poet Andrew Schelling about his work as a translator.[65]

---

64 Shainberg, Lawrence. "Exorcising Beckett," in *Writers At Work, The Paris Review Interviews*. Ninth Series, edited by George Plimpton, N.Y.: Penguin Books, 1992, p. 14.
65 Schelling, Andrew. "Mirabai's Religion of Forest & Field," in Lee Lozowick, *Death of a Dishonest Man: Poems and Prayers to Yogi Ramsuratkumar*. Prescott, Arizona: Hohm Press, 1998, p. 66

It is much the same when one comments upon the poetry of another. To summarize a poet's life work is like attempting to grasp a river that is, at the moment, branching out into new tributaries. Commentary is dangerous, albeit potentially enlivening.

Do not be disturbed, then, that there is rare linearity to the teachings that follow; do not be discouraged that later poems sometimes seem to contradict earlier poems. In a poem written in the 1980s, for example, Lee may be marveling at his full absorption in his Father, Yogi Ramsuratkumar. In another, written in early 2000, he may still beg for this grace. These are teachings contained within the medium of ecstatic speech. They are poems – the "twilight" language referred to by Andrew Schelling. Everything is relative to the moment, and to the mood of love in which the poet finds himself.

Still, despite inconsistencies for the logical mind, there is enormous value here, *and* an extensive and systematic teaching about working with mind and emotions. In presenting the following, then, I offer Lee's own words, supplemented with a few underlinings or highlightings that may guide the reader in using these poems for the purposes outlined above. **DDM** refers to the first volume of poetry, *Death of a Dishonest Man*; **GAV** refers to the second volume, *Gasping for Air in a Vacuum*.

Teachings on Mind and Emotions

1. Failure of Logical Mind

The logical mind is not the measure of this Path, lee says in this poem from 1996. The scholars and pundits who worship this rational mind will ultimately end up with hands full of stones and illusions, while the lovers, governed by the heart, will dwell in the land of Faith and Devotion. Which approach will we choose?

The skeptics and cynics say
    that Devotion is out of date
in these modern times.
    Such people say that science
is the new religion
    and that technical proof of God
is an immanent discovery.
    These contemporary pundits
say Faith is a superstition
    and that we must consider facts
coolly, analytically and rationally.
    They idolize the logical mind,
applying mathematical formulae
    to the nature of the Heart.
This is lee lozowick,
    the true heart-son
of Yogi Ramsuratkumar, Who is
    the inspirer of Faith and Devotion,
the Seat of Tradition and Truth,
    and the dispeller of illusion and lies.
This is lee lozowick,
    His crazy Heretic and arrogant Fool,
praising Him for being
    a dirty Beggar and a mad Sinner.
Let them say what they will,
    let them wander barren fields,
seeing lush countryside
    where there is only stone.
Let them claim substance

where there is only mirage.
There will always be the lost
    and always be those who find.
The Father of this little sinner
    is a beacon of Light,
brilliant and illuminating
    to the nomads of God.
Let Him draw those faithful
    to Himself, as moth to flame,
while His son this bad Poet
    rants and rages and raves
but still worships Him
    with adoration firmly rooted
in Faith and Devotion,
    heresies to a world gone mad.
lee will not suppress
    this joy because
it is not socially acceptable!
    You have broken his heart
and resurrected Faith and Devotion
    in place of the illusions
which You have so effectively
    shattered.
lee is quite unconcerned, Father.
    This is all Your problem!
– GAV, July 13, 1996

2. Yogi Ramsuratkumar's Name – A Tool for Working with the Mind

Herein Lee describes the everyday conditions of our minds and hearts. And here he presents the simple solution to it all.

The mind sets up expectations and projections,
    solidifies, crystallizes and rigidifies them,
and then defends them against intrusion,
    even of truth or reality.
We live in a dream, refusing to awaken,
    and come to believe that the dream is real.
Thank God we have you, Yogi Ramsuratkumar.
    You soften the hard wall of our fortress,
You round the sharp edges, You melt the ice
    of our resistance, You pierce our hearts
    with Your Love.
You, fiercest of warriors, most skillful
    Divine Diplomat,
    You are our hope and our need.,
without You we are lost in our vanity
    and blindness, believing ourselves to be
even wiser than the almighty Creator Himself.
    Oh You, most sweet and compassionate
Lord and Father, we bow before You with gratitude
    and awe for Your sacrifice on our behalves.
You call us home from our endless wandering
    in the wilderness of illusion, faithlessness
    and confusion.
You comfort us with affection, understanding
    and Your ever-flowing Grace and Blessings.
You warm us with the fire of Your Regard
    and Mercy, keeping us safe from harm.
We play at Your Feet, like happy children, secure and
    unconcerned with problems and life ahead
and You care for us, the ever-mindful Father
    that Your Father has given to us.
You give us Your Name, Yogi Ramsuratkumar,

to inspire us and to brighten our lives.
Truly, You are most gracious, generous and good,
    and truly, we are fortunate beyond measure
to have found You and crawled to Your door.
    This is Your true heart-son, lee lozowick,
Praising You effusively and revealing Your Madness
to the world, Your world, though most don't know it.
And this is Your wild Heretic and little sinner,
    aglow with the Radiance of You, oh Sun of God.
– GAV, 25 December 1999

This same theme was presented in an earlier poem, in
which Lee referred to himself as a "little beggar":

You know Father, Yogi Ramsuratkumar,
    Your bad Poet of a son has high aspirations.
In fact he would like nothing more
    than to serve Your Work
in whatever ways You would wish.
    Then there is the monkey-mind,
who's aspirations are of a different sort.
    The mind wants fame, recognition,
a throne for the great devotee
    of the greatest dirty Beggar who
ever existed in and out of time and space.
    The monkey-mind wants adulation.
lee says, somewhere between these two aspirations,
    "Yes, the little beggar can stay
totally detached amidst the furor of the world."
    But it really matters not,
for Your Benediction permeates it all.
    It is You who act here,

You who pretend to still be lee,
   even though that one has disappeared long ago.
So there is no fear of betrayal here,
   Your Work, Your Will is already assured.
Let Your wild Heretic tell You now,
   and with complete and total certitude:
"Your bad Poet of a son will do nothing
   but serve Your Work
in whatever ways You wish."
   So place him at the front
or hidden away in the corner,
   it is of no real concern to lee.
As long as Your Work benefits,
   this heart leaps with gladness
and these eyes mist with tears of love,
   gratitude and awe.
And never will Your Name be distant
   but echoing in every cell of Your son's body,
in every thought of his mind
   and sung joyously with his quavering voice.
– DDM, August 30, 1997

3. Effort Needed in Placing Attention

   In this next poem Lee reports on a dream he had "the other night." The dream obviously impressed him strongly, as he not only wrote a poem about it, but also used it as the subject of a talk he gave to his students soon after it happened. The poem reminds us that we must exert effort to keep our attention on God, or in this case, on Yogi Ramsuratkumar. Even in the dream, as Lee's attention became diverted, even for a moment, caused by the habits of monkey-mind, he became disconnected from the hand of Yogi Ramsuratkumar. Learning this most painful lesson, Lee cried out in sorrow, and ran to find his Master again, this time determined to never again let that connection be challenged.

I dreamt of You the other night,
    we were walking together
and You held my hand quite tenderly.
    We were lovers, lost in the joy of each other.
Then this monkey-mind, up to its old bad habits,
    became distracted by some insignificant
    complaint.
But soon my attention
    was ripped away from this diversion
to realize that our hands had come apart
    and You had gone on about Your Father's other
    business
without me, and leaving me to discover
    this most painful lesson.
My heart cried out in sorrow
    and my feet sped up to find You again.
How lucky Your son is,
    oh Madman Yogi Ramsuratkumar,
for this was only a dream,
    but a most important one indeed.
You have consumed this bad Poet completely
    and his actions are all but affects of You.
Even so, You have in Your Compassion
    allowed lee to love You as Father
and to blossom as Your son,
    Your servant, and Your devotee.
You are not separate from lee

who by Your grace knows this,
even though in Your Loving Play
    You may appear to be.
lee wants to hold Your hand
    and to feel Your Blessed touch
as long as You will permit this lila,
    for lee is Your own bad Poet and You are his Joy.
I cannot pretend separation from You anymore
    although it may be acted out for various reasons.
The wonder of this relationship,
    in spite of the illusion of You and I apart,
is precious to this arrogant Food
    and nectar to these mortal senses.
My attention will not drift from You Father —
    You have warned me in Dream.
I will not allow the phenomenal reverie
    that sparkles before this weak mind
to take me from Your eternal grasp
    for even a fraction of an instant.
Even though it is Your Hand
    holding Your own hand in a different form,
I will enjoy this play
    with surrender and bliss.
– DDM, July 7, 1995

* * *

Again, echoing the same theme, Lee laments that his mind is so easily distracted. He further demonstrates that supplication to Yogi Ramsuratkumar, for help in directing his mind, can also be a dynamic form of praise:

Oh Father,
      Yogi Ramsuratkumar,
You are consuming Your son,
      this arrogant Fool.
You are lee's heart, his muscles,
      You are his blood, his bones,
but still this bad Poet fights
      in his monkey mind.
When lee thinks of You
      the mind melts at Your Feet,
but then so quickly jumps
      to some useless distraction.
Ask Your Father in Heaven
      to Bless Your unworthy son
that lee's mind may rest
      only on You, only with You,
to be totally consumed,
      no separation at all.
This is the prayer
      of the son of Yogi Ramsuratkumar.
– DDM, Oct. 1993

4. A Serene Mind Is Not Lee's Everyday Experience

The poet flatly states that he is amazed when he hears others speak so easily about being in a place of pure peace, serenity, or "no mind." He wonders and reflects that this is *not* his daily experience. Yet, he says, these states of peace and empty mind *are available* to him. In fact, he catches glimpses of these states, and they whirl around him like clouds on a windy day so that he can speak about them to those who ask. Moreover, those to whom he speaks seem to find his answers both profound and useful. Lee ascribes all of this to the work of Yogi Ramsuratkumar, whom he says has taken him over so completely that Lee's speech is really the reflection of the Divine Beggar's speech through him. Using the phrase, "As lee becomes more irrelevant to himself," he is giving a powerful teaching about his relationship to his mind and emotions.

I hear so many teachers
    refer to themselves
in most amazing ways:
    "I am always happy," or
"I have no mind, all is perfect stillness," or
    "I know God and I am at peace."
And on and on and on.
    This is awesome to Your son
for he knows no such things.
    Joy, love, peace of mind, serenity,
Faith, surrender, purity?
    Worthy qualities all, but
not my experiences (except
    perhaps for a rare moment here or there).
And yet all of these things
    become manifest in the most excellent
ways, swirling like clouds in the wind,
    all around this arrogant Fool.
And when lee talks,
    does it seem he knows these things?
Why, yes most certainly.
    Seekers are inspired, and
absolutely sure they have
    just heard truth.
This is a successful ministry

but it is no thanks to me.
It is all You, of course.
   As lee becomes more irrelevant to himself
(Ah, a severe blow to arrogance!),
   You, Your Wisdom, Your Profound
and sacred Qualities can blossom
   here in the flower bed
of Your son's fertile heart.
   I don't even know that,
a receptive heart,
   except by inference
for You could not be so Present,
   could not flow so unrestrainedly,
were that not the case.
   Is it not so?
When Your child wonders, Dear Father,
   in that small bit of lee that remains,
Whether You will give him these things,
   Peace, love joy, Faith and surrender,
and so on, he laughs
   in the face of such madness
and says, "No, do not give me those things,
   but take away any remnants of me
and leave only You."
   Only You, Lord Yogi Ramsuratkumar. Only
You.
Your own forehead (appearing as lee's)
   deeply pranaming in the dust to You,
touching one of those rare moments
   of Love and Peace, all Praise to Your Blessings.
– DDM, March 6, 1998

* * *

In a similar vein, lee asks for madness above peace of mind:

Oh Father,
　　Yogi Ramsuratkumar,
it is madness itself
　　to ask for this Madness of Yours.
If Your son
　　was not such an arrogant Fool
he would ask for something sane
　　like success or peace of mind or health,
but lee is the son
　　of Your Father, after all.
So as You asked
　　of his Father and received,
Your son asks of You:
　　Madness for this bad Poet.
– DDM. Oct. 1993

5. Unperturbed – A Relaxed Approach

As Lee's student and devotee, I am constantly struck with
the dichotomy of acting as if I've got to discipline something
into existence, like a peaceful mind and balanced emotions,
when the reality that Lee and Yogi Ramsuratkumar embody
is that *only God is*. What silly rituals of obsession I enact
when I don't allow this teaching to soak in to the core of
my being. Instead, I often find myself marching around the
room like a good little soldier, doing some practice, while
the Lord of Heaven is reclined on my couch, watching my
drill, and patiently waiting.

... What to do, what to do, oh Light?

Persist, dig deeper, try harder
   and above all, relax, and let You do Your Work
on us and in us, above, below, beyond
   and around us, to let You have Your Way
to allow our hearts to melt with love,
   and more crucially, to allow our crystallized
mechanicality to soften and meld, to meld
   itself to Your Instruction and Your Word ..."
– GAV, February 5, 2003

6. Still Needs Work? – No Problem!

In this poem, written in December 2002, Lee testifies that, while his heart and body always immediately respond to the call of the Divine, in the person of his Master, Yogi Ramsuratkumar, his mind still needs work to get it "in order."

Specifying what he means by this "order" he clarifies that, although he never argues with Yogi Ramsuratkumar, still his "dog-donkey mind" exhibits "ignorance and childishness" when it comes to others in the world. Lee confesses that he still has trouble seeing all other forms as being completely one with that One.

Here, as everywhere in the poetry, Lee lays out his confession without any implication of self-loathing. Rather, he refers to this "problem" of mind as no more than a "petty complaint," one more circumstance to notice and reference his Father; one more excuse for praise. He addresses this "complaint" for only one reason: he wants order within his mind so that he can serve "You" – Yogi Ramsuratkumar.

You call, lee's heart and body answer,
   without hesitation or question.
But the mind? Well Father, that could still use

a few solid slaps on the back
by Your well-trained, accurate and Divine Hand.
    The mind, which never ever argues
with You, with You as Yogi Ramsuratkumar,
    still kicks up some dust now and then
in relationship to others or to the world
    in general, misunderstanding in its ignorance
and childishness that those very others
    and that very world in general is You.
Yes, is You absolutely and fully.
    So You have obedience because it is
the heart and the body which move
    instantly and effectively in response to Your call,
and this, lee lozowick, Your little beggar,
    little sinner, little madman and little little,
beggarly, sinful and mad, asks You to get this mind
    in order so he can serve You
with that too, as well as with body and heart.
    Yes, get this dog-donkey mind in order
so it can give every ounce of energy
    to the other which is You as well
as to the You which is You, which it does
    with great ease, flair and devotion.
Okay Father, Yogi Ramsuratkumar,
    this is lee lozowick, grateful
in spite of his petty complaints,
    and ever Faithful in spite of this
ridiculous mind of mentality, prostrate
    at Your sweet and Holy Feet
and covering his head with the dust
    of Your footsteps, cranky and full of You.
– GAV, 28 December 2002

7. The "Fault" of Yogi Ramsuratkumar

Here, in a traditional Hindu poetic form of *nitya stuti* –
ironical praise – Lee laments the condition of his mind and
begs for mercy from the "dirty Beggar" who "tortures" him,
and thus seemingly withholds from his devotee the complete
absorption that Lee seeks.

Oh Father of great patience,
    Yogi Ramsuratkumar,
Your son, who knows
    that You are all,
appeals to Your sense
    of Justice and Compassion.
This is the dilemma
    I place at Your Feet:
In morning meditation
    I think of sleep, or food,
and during the day
    I dream of all manner of things.
Oh dirty Beggar,
    controller of the Universe,
why do You torture Your son
    with thoughts other than You?
Why do You allow him to consider
    such mundane affairs?
I know You can turn this errant mind
    to You and only You.
Well do it and be quick about it!
    lee grows weary
with even the smallest of
    separations from You.
– DDM, August 13, 1994

8. Is Yogi Ramsuratkumar "Thinking" Through Lee?

You know Father,
    I don't think much about the future.
There is so much to do now:
    so much suffering, so many who truly need Your
Blessings.
I am quite busy enough
    with all the Work You have given.
There is certainly no time
    to indulge idle thoughts,
though once this was
    Your son's favorite pastime.
But every now and then
    a small moth of a thought
flutters almost imperceptibly
    into this silly Fool's monkey mind:
will You still consume me with Love
    whenever I think of You
and whenever I don't,
    as long as the Universe exists?
I will always be Your son,
    for that is written by Your Father in Heaven.
Will You always welcome me home
    as You have done so generously before?
Pardon Your greedy and selfish son Father,
    but You have wounded my heart You see.
I only think these things
    when You allow them.
Or is it You who thinks these things
    through the medium of Your son's eager mind?
– DDM, March 31, 1995

9. *Those Who Love the Lord Are Consumed, Body and Mind*

Oh great devouring Majesty,
    Yogi Ramsuratkumar,
Your Father has taught You well.
    You are a Master of Your craft.
And what is it
    that You are so accomplished at?
You consume the minds and hearts
    of those who love You,
leaving not even one crumb
    remaining, believing itself separate.
Your son is gone Father,
    no one left, no lee.
You have turned him into
    a bad Poet and a Renegade.
The selfish man-boy
    desiring Your Praise is no more.
You have eaten and digested him
    leaving only You.
Yes, Your Father has taught You well.
    Will You pass on these lessons
to Your Faithful son,
    so he may in turn leave no one
amongst his many companions?
    Only You, only You, Father.
– DDM, April 29, 1996

* * *

Lee is fully consumed by Yogi Ramsuratkumar:

I write You these Poems,
    Father Yogi Ramsuratkumar,
but the question is: Who is this
    I who so shamelessly claims
to be Your true heart-son,
    Your wild Heretic, and the pole
of Your Teaching and Work
    in the Western world?
This I is no-I.
    Yes, that is who I is: No-I.
The little sinner says the word, I,
    but he is under no presumption
that he is anyone or anything specific.
    There is no identification
with this I as I, while there is
    the knowledge, all the result
of Your Blessings, of this I
    as no-I, empty of all but You.
And since You are no-one
    and nothing but Father in Heaven,
well, we will leave the implications
    for those who love philosophy and debate.
In any event, Father of Mercy, I
    just wanted to assure You
that Your lee lozowick, Your I,
    in this case was only no-I.
No-I throws himself, itself, in Your Path,
    not separate from that upon which You tread.
– GAV, 3 November 1999

* * *

May all who read these words be relieved, to some small degree at least, of the suffering created by their identification with mind and emotions. For, as Lee said in 1997, "There's only ever one problem – an unwillingness to radically confront the need to cease all identifications."

Lee Lozowick
"As He Is"

The excerpt that comprises this Appendix is taken from Lee's most recent journal, titled *The Little Book of Lies and Other Myths*, and credited: "by Lee Lozowick, liar and mythmaker" (Hohm Press, 2005). This excerpt is included here to give readers a taste of Lee Lozowick *"uncut."* He wrote this himself, and did not allow anyone to edit anything – not even a comma. He allowed no changes to spelling, grammar or capitalization. He had his own purposes in putting out the straight, uncensored version of his mind, heart, outrageous sense of humor and integrated wisdom in a way that transcended the need for political or grammatical correctness.

As Lee's editor for the present book, *Feast or Famine*, I was working from his spoken transcripts. It was therefore my decision where to punctuate his phrases, what to cut and where, and what to group together into the various subject areas. Throughout, I also used standard spelling, capitalization and punctuation.

Although I attempted to give readers the flavor and mood of Lee's verbal presentations, my own editorial biases certainly shape the final product. It is almost inevitable that this would happen, which creates a somewhat terrifying responsibility for an editor working on her spiritual Master's testimonies.

At the same time, he chose to use me as his scribe in this project, and for this I can only be grateful.

Because the following piece relates to the mind it should be useful and enjoyable to readers of this current book. You are urged to read more of Lee "uncut" by going to the other journals:

Volume I. *Eccentricities, Idiosyncrasies And Sacred Utterances From A Contemporary Western Baul.* (Hohm Press, 1990)

Volume II. *In The Style Of Eccentricities, Idiosyncrasies And Sacred Utterances from a Contemporary Western Baul.* (Hohm Press, 1992)

Volume III. *In The Mood Of "In The Style Of Eccentricities, Idiosyncrasies And Sacred Utterances From A Contemporary Western Baul"* (Hohm Press, 1994)

Volume IV. *Cranky Rants and Bitter Wisdom from One Considered Wise in Some Quarters* (Hohm Press, 2002)

Volume V. *The Little Book of Lies and Other Myths* (Hohm Press, 2005)

In 1993, after Lee had written two of the five journals, I was traveling with the group that accompanied him to Europe. One night I was in charge of selling books and approached Lee with a question. Many people had come to the book table and asked me "Which book is best?" or "Which book should I read first?" When I related these inquiries to Lee he gestured to the books piled on one side of the table, saying, "Tell them these are all *about* the Teaching." Then he pointed specifically to the two journals: "Tell them these *are* the Teaching."

* * *

5 July 2005

I awoke this morning with another catchy phrase, not for the path itself, but definitely useful for a facet of practice: "mind mosquitos." You know, those annoying, buzzing little (and often malarial) thoughts that keep irritating you with their ever-presence, like "Oh, the way he looked at me...," and "It was that tone of voice she always uses that..", or "that was so manipulative (cruel, aggressive, ugly, hurtful, vindictive, predictable, effete, arrogant, vain, undignified, inelegant, purposeful, etc., etc...)..." Yeah, those not-so subtle little arrows of poison that turn you away from people (and things: "that movie was just like all movies...," or "Indian food is always...," and "hmm, people who dress like that..." and bias any objectivity you may possibly have. And they're always around regardless of the season, too bad, they don't die in winter. I suppose if we wanted to go on we could also talk about the "mind-ghosts" which are the also ever-present thoughts but the invisible ones, the ones below the horizon of awareness, the ones that perversely affect and toxify it all, that define our cynical, or superior, or violent, or self-hating, or sarcastic or whatever, world view, the underlying thoughts and motives that move us, that define our tacit seperative view of our lives and circumstances, that keep us insular, isolated and deep in illusion, that are what continue, like clockwork, to keep us chronically and absolutely predictably mechanical. And then there are the "mind mice," the thoughts that nibble away at all the inspiration to be different, to practice, to change our neurotic behavior, the "you don't have to practice because it's all already perfect, just as it is", and "nothing ever works for me, I try and try and it's all just so useless," or "why even bother putting effort into anything, they'll just drop a bomb and destroy everything anyway" thoughts that keep us well under their thumbs (they have many, more than humans). Yeah, watch out for those "mind-mice", they leave little shit pellets everywhere, all full of bacteria and if you don't treat the results of the existence of these, all of these, pests, the effects can be quite bad, infection, fever, dis-ease, all manner of affliction. So be on your guard when the mind-mosquitos buzz, kill them immediately (or if you're conscious enough, let them suck so much blood that they explode, killing themselves—yes—it works) and banish the mind-ghosts, free them from their ghost-realms, and let them move on and trap the mind-mice and finish them off (the use of certain odors to keep them away is also effective, at least usually as we had a plague of skunks on our Ashram once and someone said if we could get lion scat, that's shit, and put it all around, the "lion-vibes" would definitely scare off the skunks so we, as luck would have it, have a zoo just minutes from us, which zoo, which further luck would have it, has lions, which lions, which nature would have it, shit with zoo-keeper relieving regularly, which those very zoo-keepers were happily willing to give to us, which shit, furthermore, we spread liberally around the skunk domains, which skunks completely ignored the shit and went on about their business as if they knew full well that we had tried to trick them and that there were no real, live lions anywhere even close (except locked up behind bars and very highly unlikely to chase down and eat skunks anyway, which skunks most certainly not smelling like gazelles or gnus, which knowledge of said skunks, by the way, not creating any self-hatred or weak self-confidence in their psychology at all, in fact they tend to be extremely pretentious.). And what's your inner animal?

INDEX

A

abidharma, 24

"accept what is . . .," 37, 46, 11, 115, 124, 137, 142, 170-171; *also see* "as it is"

acceptance, 106, 134-135

active(ly) passive (Desjardins), 36, 124

Advaita Vedanta, 54

aggression, 3, 7, 16, 53, 92

aim, *see* "articulate your___"

alcoholic, 21-22

Ali, Mohammed, 37

ancestors 40-41

anger, 46, 121, 130, 135, 149, 170, 178

angry, 3, 121, 126, 130, 136

"articulate your aim," 25-29

"as it is," 32-35, 47, 56, 61, 81, 110, 114, 128, 132-134, 143, 152-153, 165, 183; *also see* "accept what is . . ."

As It Is (Young), 60-66, 172

ashram, 19-20, 26, 33, 74, 85, 181,182; *also see* Hauteville

assertion, 46, 83, 85, 91; *also see* "Just This"

astrological chart, 40, 43

attachment(s), 24, 30, 31-33, 72, 76, 79-80

attention
on children, 99
on context, 153
on God, 193-196
managing, 97-105
on the source, 104-105
on toes, 102-103
also see paying attention; training

Aurobindo, Sri, 184-186

awareness / unawareness, 15, 19, 24, 174; *also see* consciousness

B

bands, xv, xvii

basic goodness (Chögyam Trungpa), 98

Bauls, 81, 90

Beckett, Samuel, 187

Beloved, 58-59

body
affected by emotion, 119
chemistry, 101, 164
image, 169
observing the, 146-147
toxic, 161, 163-164
work with the, 44

Bond, James, 96

Bowie, David, 76-77

"box," the, 89

Bryant, Kobe, 71-72

Buddha, 9, 70, 161, 171

Buddhism, xiv, 4, 11, 24, 55, 71, 81, 114, 165; *also see* Trungpa Rinpoche; *Dakini's Warm Breath*; *dzogchen*; Tibetan; Vajrayana

Bukowski, Charles, xiii

Bush, George, 162

C

Castaneda, Carlos, 53-54, 60, 66

catharsis, 148-150

cathexis, 148-150

cell phones, 162

Chaitanya, 81

change, 20, 47, 83, 90, 94, 101-102, 104, 106, 135, 144, 147, 169

chant, 11, 143,183

character(s) (E.J. Gold), 34-35, 95, 96

chart, *see* astrological chart

chemical reactions, *see* body

chief feature (Gurdjieff), 26, 98

chief weakness (Gurdjieff), *see* chief feature

child's mind, *see* mind

Index

Index

Index

OTHER BOOKS BY LEE LOZOWICK

GETTING REAL
by Lee Lozowick

This book contains teachings from a seminar given in Mexico City in May 2006. Lee speaks about and actively demonstrates what it means to "get real," in contrast to the illusions of what it means to be "spiritual" in this day and age. His words are compassionate, but often brutally honest and humorous. He confronts the notions that keep his students and listeners stuck in their impractical visions of God or enlightened life. Instead, he encourages a relationship to reality that is characterized by integrity and discipline.
Paper, $16.95, 160 pages, ISBN: 978-1-890772-76-5

THE ALCHEMY OF TRANSFORMATION
by Lee Lozowick   Foreword by: Claudio Naranjo, M.D.

A concise and straightforward overview of the principles of spiritual life as developed and taught by Lee Lozowick since 1975. Subjects of use to seekers and serious students of any spiritual tradition include a radical, elegant and irreverent approach to the possibility of change from ego-centeredness to God-centeredness—the ultimate human transformation.
Paper, $14.95, 192 pages, ISBN: 978-0-934252-62-1

THE ALCHEMY OF LOVE AND SEX
by Lee Lozowick   Foreword by Georg Feuerstein, Ph.D.

Reveals 70 "secrets" about love, sex and relationships. Advocating neither asceticism nor hedonism, Lee Lozowick presents a middle path—one grounded in the appreciation of simple human relatedness. Topics include: * what men want from women in sex, and what women want from men * the development of a passionate love affair with life * how to balance the essential masculine and essential feminine * the dangers and possibilities of sexual Tantra * the reality of a genuine, sacred marriage, and much more.

"... attacks Western sexuality with a vengeance."
—*Library Journal.*

Paper, 312 pages, $16.95, ISBN: 978-0-934252-58-4

CONSCIOUS PARENTING
by Lee Lozowick

Any individual who cares for children needs to attend to the essential message of this book: that the first two years are the most crucial time in a child's education and development, and that children learn to be healthy and "whole" by living with healthy, whole adults.

Offers practical guidance and help for anyone who wishes to bring greater consciousness to every aspect of childraising, including: * conception, pregnancy and birth * emotional development * language usage * role modeling: the mother's role, the father's role * the exposure to various influences * establishing workable boundaries, and * the choices we make on behalf on our children's education.

Paper, $17.95, 378 pages, ISBN: 978-0-934252- 67-6

DERISIVE LAUGHTER FROM A BAD POET
Excerpts from the Teaching of An American Baul
by Lee Khépa Baul   Foreword by Claudio Naranjo, M.D.

True to the itinerant spirit of the Baul, Lee Lozowick (Khépa Baul) has been travelling regularly to Europe since 1986. This book grew out of an expressed desire, particularly from his audiences in Germany, to read his words in their own native language. With translations in both French and German, each excerpt opens another window, offering the perceptive reader a glimpse of one of the many moods of this Bad Poet and a vision of the expansive nature of the dharma of this spiritual Master. Topics range from the nature of prayer and the Grace of loving God, to the illness of contemporary culture and the unique challenge of building genuine community as an alternative.
Paper, 80 pages, $8.95, ISBN: 978-0-934252-36-2

THE ONLY GRACE IS LOVING GOD
by Lee Lozowick

Love, God, Loving God, Grace, Divine Will—these subjects have engaged the minds and hearts of theologians throughout the ages, and even caused radical schisms within organized religions. Lee Lozowick dares to address them again, and in a way entirely original. He challenges all conventional definitions of love, and all superficial assumptions about the nature of loving God, and introduces a radical distinction which he calls the "whim of God" to explain why the random and beneficent Grace of loving God is humanity's ultimate possibility. More than just esoteric musings, *The Only Grace is Loving God* is an urgent and practical appeal to every hungry heart.
Paper, 108 pages, $5.95, ISBN: 978-0-934252-07-2

LIVING GOD BLUES
by Lee Lozowick

This book is the first exposition of an experiment in both intentional community-living and spiritual practice that has been going on in the United States and Europe for more than thirty years. Focused around the author's teaching work, the Hohm Community has grown from a handful of friends and students to a culture of several hundred men, women and children. Drawing from its roots among the Bauls—or Bards of Bengal—a rag-tag bunch of musicians, ecstatic poets and lovers of God, this community of Western Bauls share an eclectic approach to spiritual life, drawing from all the great religious traditions—Sahajia Buddhism, Vaishnava Hinduism, esoteric Christianity, and others. Introductory sections, written by senior students, describe the spiritual practices of the community and spell out principal tenets of the Master's teaching—such as the idea that "God does not live in the sky."

Paper, 168 pages, $9.95, ISBN: 978-0-934252-09-6

LAUGHTER OF THE STONES
by Lee Lozowick

Wise teachers have always used laughter as one effective tool in preparing the student's heart for essential instruction. In this refreshing book, Lee offers his humor, piercing sarcasm, and practical wisdom in a series of classic essays including: "How Not to Act Superior When You Really Are," and "The Divine Path of Growing Old." A necessary book for any *serious*, spiritual student.

Paper 140 pages, $9.95, ISBN: 978-0-934252-00-3

THE CHEATING BUDDHA
by Lee Lozowick

The necessity for a spirituality grounded in the body and relevant to the times in which we live is the thread that ties together the essays in this book. Lee Lozowick writes here about the nature of human communication/ communion; compassion for others, and the fantasies vs. the realities of enlightenment. A book of living words, full of earthy wisdom.

Paper, 144 pages, $7.95, ISBN: 978-0-934252-03-4

IN THE FIRE
by Lee Lozowick

This book addresses the issues that arise in every student's relationship with a spiritual Master: service, friendship, surrender, obedience, humor, devotion and faith. A clear and readily-usable foundation for practice, *In The Fire* will bring seekers face-to-face with their own questions, resistances and fears. It will also substantiate their heartfulness and longing.

Paper, 264 pages, $9.95, ISBN: 978-0-895560-02-5

ACTING GOD
by Lee Lozowick

Can humanity be saved from hunger, fear, its own suicidal tendencies? Is it possible to create a new culture of sanity and enlightenment? An eminently practical book which addresses these questions, offering not only ideas, but definitive means to disentangle our priorities and redirect our focus to the "bottom-line" of spiritual life.

Paper, 64 pages, $5.95, ISBN: 978-0-934252-05-8

THE YOGA OF ENLIGHTENMENT/
THE BOOK OF UNENLIGHTENMENT
by Lee Lozowick

Enlightenment, contrary to popular misconceptions, is much more than the experience of the "heaven-realm" of bliss and light. To fully grasp the reality of enlightenment is only possible when one is willing to embrace the other side—the not-knowing, the ignorance, and the darkness. The balance and interdependence of paradoxes is the basis of this book.

Paper, 240 pages, $9.95, ISBN: 978-0-934252-06-5

DEATH OF A DISHONEST MAN
Poems And Prayers To Yogi Ramsuratkumar
by Lee Lozowick

This book is the living witness of a rare relationship between Master and disciple. It catalogs the devotional poetry—often written in the classic form of *ninda stuti*, "ironical praise"—of Lee Lozowick addressed to his Master, the Divine Beggar of Tiruvannamalai, Yogi Ramsuratkumar. Beginning with Lee's initial expressions of love and surrender in May 1979, hundreds more poems followed. This book contains those written through March 1998.

The essential poems and prayers are augmented with dharmic essays by other renowned individuals, including Arnaud Desjardins, Claudio Naranjo, Robert Svoboda and poet Andrew Schelling. Commentaries by some of Lee's students and dozens of Lee's song lyrics complete this bountiful offering.

Hardcover, 1276 pages, $108.00 ISBN: 978-0-934252-87-4

GASPING FOR AIR IN A VACUUM
Poems And Prayers To Yogi Ramsuratkumar
by Lee Lozowick

Following in the format of *Death of a Dishonest Man* the poetry contained in this book spans the period from April 1998 through May 2004. Although Yogi Ramsuratkumar left his physical body in February 2001, Lee has continued to praise Him day and night, and these poems reveal the union that flourishes and deepens between the Father and his "true heart son." To read these poems and prayers is to glimpse the reality of non-duality. Sometimes tender and intimate, at other times searing in their indictment of the fickleness of the Master's devotees, these poems promise an introduction to the house of prayer.

Essays included by Arnaud Desjardins, Llewellyn Vaughan-Lee, John Welwood, John Friend, Petri Murien, and others. Many more lyrics and two CDs of Lee's rock operas (*The Nine House of Mila* and *John T.*). A sumptuous feast.

Hardcover; 1099 pages; $145.00 ISBN: 978-1-890772-45-1

108 POEMS AND PRAYERS TO YOGI RAMSURATKUMAR
by Lee Lozowick   Translation by Vincent & Adeline Vigor

English and French edition
This book is the result of a growing hunger among Lee Lozowick's French students, and French-speaking devotees of Yogi Ramsuratkumar, to read Lee's poetry to the Blessed Beggar in their own language. One-hundred-eight of Lee's previously published poems (from *Death of a Dishonest Man*) are contained herein, chosen for their representation of the

many moods of love in which the devotee sings to his Master. These translations keep the intention of being as faithful as possible to the style of the "bad Poet" (as Lee calls himself), and eminently convey the wild, vibrant and spontaneous energy that the original English versions offer.

Hardcover, 310 pages, color photos, $50.00 ISBN: 978-1-890772-53-6

The Journals of Lee Lozowick (Volumes 2-5)

The living teaching of the American-born spiritual master, Lee Lozowick, the instigator of the Western Baul Tradition, is here expressed and encoded in 5 volumes (only 4 are still available) of his personal journals. Each book contains thirty or more of Lee's spontaneous essays (he tells the reader that no editing is made) written one-a-day over the course of several months at a time, beginning in 1990 and culminating in 2005.

Commenting upon these writings, Lee remarked that everything prior to these books that was credited to him was "about the teaching." With the publication of these journals he said, "These *are* the teaching." No linear continuity will be found herein. These books capture the mind, heart and mood of the spiritual Master as he reflects upon life *as it is*. They are guaranteed to (choose one or more): a.) provoke, b.) delight, c.) outrage, d.) frustrate, e.) enlighten, f.) all of the above.

VOLUME 1: ECCENTRICITIES, IDIOSYNCRASIES, AND SACRED UTTERANCES.
OUT OF PRINT

VOLUME 2: IN THE STYLE OF THE ECCENTRICITIES, IDIOSYNCRASIES AND SACRED UTTERANCES OF A CONTEMPORARY WESTERN BAUL

by Mr. Lee Khépa Baul

May 10, 1992 through July 17, 1992

Hardcover, 198 pages, $35.00, ISBN: 978-0-934252-34-8

VOLUME 3: IN THE MOOD OF "IN THE STYLE OF THE ECCENTRICITIES, IDIOSYNCRASIES AND SACRED UTTERANCES OF A CONTEMPORARY WESTERN BAUL"

by Mr. Lee Khépa Baul

(October 31, 1993 through March 7, 1994)

Hardcover, 168 pages, $35.00, ISBN: 978- 0-934252-43-0

VOLUME 4: CRANKY RANTS AND BITTER WISDOM FROM ONE CONSIDERED WISE IN SOME QUARTERS

by Lee Lozowick

(February 27, 2002 through May 12, 2002)

Hardcover, 232 pages, $50.00, ISBN: 978-1-890772-29-1

VOLUME 5: THE LITTLE BOOK OF LIES AND OTHER MYTHS

by Lee Lozowick, liar and mythmaker

(May 14, 2005 through July 19, 2005)

Hardcover, 255 pages, $50.00, ISBN: 978-1-890772-58-1

MUSIC BY LEE LOZOWICK

ECRASE PAR L'AMOUR (CRUSHED BY LOVE)
by Lee Lozowick

Lee Lozowick has been writing provocative and tender lyrics, singing in public and recording for over twenty years, first with Arizona-based rock and roll band, *Liars, Gods and Beggars*, then with the internationally acclaimed blues group *Shri*, and most recently with the Lee Lozowick Project. On this solo album, Lee's voice emerges with freshness, passion, depth and texture, thanks to the superb musical composition and production of collaborator Paul Durham (formerly of *Black Lab*). His lyrics are at once heartbreaking and hopeful, shocking and prayerful. A powerful mix.

1 CD, 12 tracks, 50 minutes, $15.00

L'ANGE BRISE (BROKEN ANGEL)
by Lee Lozowick

This second solo album by Lee Lozowick stands on the powerful shoulders of his previous *ecrase par l'amour*, with more devastating cries to heaven. Taking his work to the next level, these new compositions will leave listeners alternately discomforted and longing for more. His bold lyrics hold nothing back, as he declaims the illusions of contemporary culture, while at the same time recalling timeless values of love, family, and surrender to God. This compilation will provoke both contemplation and the desire for radical action.

1 CD, 12 tracks, 46 minutes, $15.00

OTHER TITLES OF INTEREST
FROM HOHM PRESS

AS IT IS
A Year on the Road with a Tantric Teacher
by M. Young

A first-hand account of a one-year journey around the world in the company of *tantric* teacher, Lee Lozowick. This book catalogues the trials and wonders of day-to-day interactions between a teacher and his students, and presents a broad range of his teachings given in seminars from San Francisco, California to Rishikesh, India. *As It Is* considers the core principles of *tantra*, including non-duality, compassion (the Bodhisattva ideal), service to others, and transformation within daily life. Written as a narrative, this captivating book will appeal to practitioners of *any* spiritual path. Readers interested in a life of clarity, genuine creativity, wisdom and harmony will find this an invaluable resource.

Paper, 840 pages, 24 b&w photos, $29.95 ISBN: 978-0-934252-99-7

ZEN TRASH
The Irreverent and Sacred Teaching Stories
of Lee Lozowick
Edited and with Commentary by Sylvan Incao

This book contains dozens of teaching stories from many world religious traditions—including Zen, Christianity, Tibetan Buddhism, Sufism and Hinduism—rendered with a twist of humor, irony or provocation by contemporary spiritual teacher Lee

Lozowick. They are compiled from thirty years of Lozowick's talks and seminars in the U.S., Canada, Europe, Mexico and India.

These stories will typically confound the mind and challenge any conventional seriousness about the spiritual path. In essence, however, they hold what every traditional teaching story has always held—the possibility of glimpsing reality, beyond the multiple illusions that surround the truth.

Paper, 150 pages, $12. 95, ISBN: 978-1-890772-21-5

YOGI RAMSURATKUMAR
Under the Punnai Tree
by M. Young

Hohm Press's first full-length biography of the wondrous and blessed beggar of Tiruvannamalai. More than 80 photographs. To be touched by the truth, beauty and love of this remarkable being will stir the heart's deepest longings. This book celebrates the inspiration of one rare individual who abandoned everything for the love of God.

Paper, 752 pages, $39.95, ISBN: 978-1-890772-34-5

ONLY GOD
A Biography Of Yogi Ramsuratkumar
by Regina Sara Ryan

"Only God" was the Yogi's creed and approach to life. His unusual innocence and radiant presence were recognized by seekers from East and West. This book includes the lives and teachings of the holy beggar's three gurus: Ramana Maharshi, Sri Aurobindo, and Swami Papa Ramdas. An enjoyable mix of storytelling, interviews and fact finding.

Hardcover, $39.95, 832 pages, ISBN: 978-1-890772-35-2

FACETS OF THE DIAMOND
Wisdom of India
by James Capellini

A book of rare and moving photographs, brief biographies, and evocative quotes from contemporary spiritual teachers in the Eastern tradition, including Ramana Maharshi, Swami Papa Ramdas, Sri Yogi Ramsuratkumar, Swami Prajnanpad, Chandra Swami, Nityananda, Shirdi Sai Baba, and Sanatan Das Baul. This mood-altering book richly captures the texture and flavor of the Eastern spiritual path and the teacher-disciple relationship, and offers penetrating insight into the lives of those who carry the flame of wisdom for the good of all humanity.

Hardcover, 240 pages, $39.95, 45 photographs ISBN: 978-0-934252-53-9

CAUGHT IN THE BELOVED'S PETTICOATS
A Treatise on the Eternal Way
by M. Young

Written in the style of a wayfarer's journal, this book chronicles the travels and teachings of Western Baul Master, Lee Lozowick, during the summer of 2005, which marked thirty years since the commencement of his teaching work. From the Southwestern desert of the U.S. to England, France and Germany, readers join the caravan of travelers with the spiritual Master, meeting him and his students in unexpected situations, both usual and extraordinary, and sharing in the insight, provocation, art, music, grace and grit in which this living teacher offers up gems of wisdom with eloquence, humor and honesty.

Paper; 692 pages; $35.00 ISBN: 978-1-890772-63-5

A MAN AND HIS MASTER
by Mani, with S. Lkasham

Yogi Ramsuratkumar is unique, even in India's long and rich tradition—and Mani was his closest servant, his trusted "right-hand man." Mani's heart and devotion shine through this touchingly personal account of his six years at the Master's side.

Paper, 394 pages, $21.95, ISBN: 978-1-890772-36-9

HALFWAY UP THE MOUNTAIN
The Error of Premature Claims to Enlightenment
by Mariana Caplan   Foreword by Fleet Maull

Dozens of first-hand interviews with students, respected spiritual teachers and masters, together with broad research are synthesized here to assist readers in avoiding the pitfalls of the spiritual path. Topics include: mistaking mystical experience for enlightenment; ego inflation, power and corruption among spiritual leaders; the question of the need for a teacher; disillusionment on the path . . . and much more.

"Caplan's illuminating book . . . urges seekers to pay the price of traveling the hard road to true enlightenment."
—*Publisher's Weekly*

Paper, 600 pages $21.95 ISBN: 978-0-934252-91-1

To Order:

Call Hohm Press at 800-381-2700, or visit us on the web: www.hohmpress.com

About the Author

Lee Lozowick is an American-born spiritual teacher who has taught thousands of people in North America, Europe and India since 1975. He is the spiritual son of the beggar-saint, Yogi Ramsuratkumar. Lee has written more than seventeen books, including: *Conscious Parenting; The Alchemy of Transformation;* and *The Alchemy of Love and Sex;* and has been translated and published in French, German, Spanish, Portuguese and other languages. He is also a poet, a lyricist, and the lead singer for both an American blues group, *SHRI*, and a European rock band, *The Lee Lozowick Project*. He lives in northern Arizona.

Contact

The author and/or the publisher can be contacted at:

Hohm Press
PO Box 2501
Prescott, Arizona, 86302

Visit Hohm Press online at: www.hohmpress.com